Motherhood
Is the New MBA

Motherhood
Is the New MBA

Using Your Parenting Skills to
Be a Better Boss

SHARI STORM

Thomas Dunne Books
St. Martin's Press
New York

THOMAS DUNNE BOOKS.
An imprint of St. Martin's Press.

www.thomasdunnebooks.com
www.stmartins.com

Book design by Rich Arnold

Library of Congress Cataloging-in-Publication Data

Storm, Shari.
   Motherhood is the new MBA : using your parenting skills to be a better boss / Shari Storm. — 1st ed.
      p. cm.
   ISBN 978-0-312-54431-7 (alk. paper)
   1. Management.   2. Motherhood.   3. Interpersonal relations.   4. Psychology, Industrial.   I. Title.
   HD31.S69635 2009
   658.4'09—dc22

                                        2009016945

First Edition: October 2009

10 9 8 7 6 5 4 3 2 1

To my three families—the Storms,
the Drummonds, and Verity

Contents

Acknowledgments

When someone asks how I could write a book while raising three small children and working as an executive, I usually joke about the things I don't do—like clean, pay bills on time, go to the gym, or make dinner.

But the truth is I never could have done any of this without the help of my friends and family. I have many blessings in my life and many people I am thankful for.

First and foremost, there is Andrea Somberg, my agent, who is as delightful as she is hardworking and talented. I am grateful for the folks at Thomas Dunne / St. Martin's Press. Thank you to my editor, Toni Plummer, for guiding me through this process; for Cynthia Merman, who did wonders with the copyediting; and for Nadea Mina, who helped get the word out.

I can't even begin to thank my siblings enough. I am eternally grateful for Kate Drummond and Stephen Williams, and Stacey Storm and Aram Pierce for their endless hours of babysitting. I am so fortunate to have my wonderful parents, Jack and Joyce Storm, and my incredible in-laws, Ron and Jean Drummond. I'm also grateful for Rob (the real talent) and Katie Drummond, who send support from across the country.

I am lucky for the exceptional grandparents I have

as role models and for all of my cousins, aunts, and uncles. I am fortunate to have the amazing women at Main Street Kids who love and nurture my children every day.

There is a special group of people who helped with the actual writing. Terrell Meek was the first person to peer into the proposal. Tracy Elfstrom not only taught me to golf, she read my first draft. Ron Shevlin gave great advice with kindness and candor. Karen Burns provided that last edit that made me finally like the manuscript.

There are the people I work with. Of course, my boss, Bill Hayes, has been a phenomenal mentor and has given me more support than most CEOs would ever dream of giving. Sherry Steckly has been my friend and confidante for more than a decade. Vivian Valencia has stuck with me all these years and keeps me enthusiastic. I appreciate Laurel McJannet for letting me use her as my first example. And Lee Oveson I thank for the postage and the perspective.

Many thanks to Jill Vicente, Danielle Salisbury, and Karen Burns for the emergency think and drink and to Denise Wymore for coming up with the title at the beginning of all this.

I give special thanks to Brent Dixon for the Web site, the creative chats, and the music. I thank Brian Stork for teaching me enough html to be dangerous (and to keep the blogs and Web sites going).

I thank Claudia Majack for holding the baby all those summer nights.

I appreciate Shane Atchison for letting me pick his brain at the start and Krista Loercher for giving me time and advice as things got rolling. I really appreciate Nicole Vandenberg and Debbie Pfeiffer for their friendship and the people they introduced me to.

Every woman I interviewed for this book taught me, inspired me, and enriched my life. But I must make special mention of Kathryn Ellison, who wrote *The Mommy Brain: How Motherhood Makes You Smarter*, and Paula Spencer, author of *Momfidence! An Oreo Never Killed Anybody and Other Secrets of Happier Parenting*.

A huge thank-you goes to my inner circle of the past two decades: Jeni Ward, Nicki Solie, Cathlyn Nedved, Kari-Mae Miles, Susan Gimbl, Dana Thomlinson, Brenda Wilner, Andrea Jones, Janine Byers, Val Chang, Angela Hoskins, Trina Wagenblast, Molly Hegenderfer, and Kari Hale.

I'm lucky to have three women who I consider lifelong friends: Sandra Alberti, Mary Anne Fisher, and Lisa Berger. Laughing with them is the best therapy for anything that ails me.

Of course, I hold my three daughters, Rebekah, Lexington, and Johanna, in the most special place for their daily inspiration. I love and cherish them more than I thought humanly possible.

And last, I thank my husband, Dave, who laughed when I first told him my idea of this book. He laughed and then said, "That is awesome and you are the perfect person to do it. When do we start?"

Motherhood
Is the New MBA

Introduction: Burp Rags Are for Sissies

I have superhuman abilities.

Well, I *had* superhuman abilities. And I'm not alone. If you've ever been pregnant—or know someone who has—you know what I am talking about.

I initially discovered my superhuman powers eight weeks into my first pregnancy. Working late one night, I stopped to drop off some papers on a colleague's desk. Upon opening the door to her office, the overpowering scent of new carpeting hit me. Funny, I thought, I don't remember seeing the memo mentioning new carpeting. And, as an executive of my company, I usually knew about such things.

I flipped on the light and looked around. Odd. No new carpet. And then I saw it. Sitting on her desk was a two-inch-by-four-inch carpet sample. It was that tiny carpet sample I had smelled so acutely.

Oh my God, I thought to myself. I have superhuman smelling capability.

And it's true. It's not at all uncommon for pregnant

women to have an amplified sense of smell. The prevailing theory is that a sharper sense of smell is an evolutionary necessity to keep us from eating anything harmful when we are most vulnerable.

For me, it was my introduction into the world of superhuman powers, borne of motherhood.

I have managed all sorts of people—call-center staff, counselors, salespeople, technical folks, marketing employees, accounting and financial types. Before I had kids, I never would have dreamed of reading a book comparing management to raising a two-year-old. Managing adults is nothing like raising kids. Adults are mature. Adults are complicated.

Then my baby turned two.

Yes, most adults are more mature than a two-year-old. Often, adults moderate their response to disappointment better than two-year-olds. But sometimes that simply means that their tantrums are more sophisticated. Adults use words and sentences to get what they want, instead of whining or puppy dog–style stares. But are adults really all that different? Some days it seems to me that the only difference between adults and toddlers is that adults have larger heads and longer arms.

I have three children now, all girls. The more I watch my daughters, the more I realize that children are simply adults who haven't yet learned to hide their feelings, temper their responses, or worry about social expectations. Two-year-olds are the perfect study in human nature.

The idea for this book came to me one day when I suspected a coworker had done something she shouldn't have. I asked her about it point-blank. Her response reminded me of something. I racked my brain. Where had I seen that look before? And then it hit me—my daughter. It was the look I had seen when I asked, "Did you put your sneakers in the oven?" or "Does your pull-up need to be changed?" My daughter often gave me this same look—the look someone gives the moment before she lies.

The look is fleeting, but it has four phases. The first part is the panic at being caught doing something you know is wrong. The second flicker is that of calculation, quickly sizing up the odds of getting found out in the lie. The third phase is the decision to jump into the lie. The last is guilt that is impossible to fully hide.

Once I recognized the parallels between raising children and managing people, I saw them everywhere. Suddenly, my pediatric books became rife with management advice and my management books contained wisdom for raising children. It all became one big cross-pollination of growth and learning for me. I realized that my training was happening twenty-four hours a day, seven days a week.

Once I realized this, I became more confident in the roles I was playing, both as a mother and as a manager. One morning, my baby spit up on my business suit just as I was walking out the door. Armed with this new confidence, I didn't change my jacket. Instead,

I changed my attitude. My new attitude goes something like this: Burp rags are for sissies.

The world needs capable women to run our companies and bolster our economy. The world needs talented women to raise our children and produce the next generation. After all, it is the next generation who will take care of the world when we are too tired to do it anymore. Right now, I am doing both. And if purple Play-Doh under my fingernails and the scent of baby puke on my blouse distracts you, well then, step away from the executive table. You aren't ready to play with the big girls.

My company has been good to me while I've had children, but there are no other mothers at my level. There are some working fathers in the top ranks, but being a working dad isn't the same. (And anyone who thinks it is has never had a boob leak in the boardroom.)

Most working moms grapple with the same issue, the mother's dilemma. No matter how hard we try, we never feel like we are doing anything well. When we are at the office, we feel guilty that we are not home with our kids; when we are home with our kids, we feel guilty that we are not at the office. It feels like our family suffers because of our job and our job suffers because of our family.

I choose not to believe this. I don't work late nights at the office because of my day-care pickup; I take more days away because of sick kids. But as a mother, I bring something unique to the party—and that something is a crucial component to the success of my company.

Every day I use certain parts of my brain in ways I never had to before. Raising children is a veritable boot camp for self-awareness, self-regulation, motivation, empathy, and social skills. I'm not talking a beautiful, peaceful, drink-tea-and-watch-the-sunrise boot camp. I'm talking army-style, train for Ironman, made-for-reality-TV boot camp. Your brain is like every other muscle in your body. If you exercise it, it will become stronger, faster, and healthier.

While it is tempting for me and those I work with to think that motherhood has made me less of a contributor at the office, it simply isn't true.

The key is to articulate the lessons learned from raising your children so that you can identify the parallels and, more important, draw self-confidence from them.

I remember the first time my "mommy-ism" crossed over into my professional life. Granted, I was sleep deprived and a bit frazzled when two of my salespeople told me about a deal they had just closed. I exclaimed, "I am sooo proud of you!" The way I said it was unmistakably mommyspeak. But both people smiled—authentic, happy smiles—particularly the fifty-year-old man. I'm certainly not advocating the use of mommy talk at the office, but it is interesting to note that it can be perceived as comforting, even to the least babylike among us.

Another time, after days of back-and-forth with a

consultant who was trying to convince me to get into the subprime mortgage business, I snapped. I had already told him why we didn't think that business line was a good idea, how it went against our corporate values, how we deemed it too risky. Finally, I just said, "We aren't doing it because I said so!" a statement, in retrospect, that probably saved many people's jobs.

Once I discovered that I *can* run the office like I run my home—with empathy, compassion, humor, fun, and even strictness—I felt empowered, emboldened! I found myself embracing my new self-confidence, owning my power. I didn't turn into a raving boss lady, but I did become much more comfortable asking for feedback, listening to all sides, and then calling the shots. I became comfortable saying, "This is how it's going to be because I said so."

I became comfortable telling people I'm proud of them. I started saying, "I have a story to tell you." I said (nicely, of course) things like, "Mind your own stuff and not your neighbors'," "Don't tattle," and unfortunately, once, "Keep your hands to yourself." When people under me act up, as people sometimes do, I remind myself that I am their boss. And just like I constantly remind myself to act like a good mom, I also remind myself to act like a good boss.

This book is a compilation of a few of the things I have learned from raising my three daughters (Rebekah, five; Lexie, three; and Johanna, one) as well as advice from more than sixty women who are mothers, managers, and mentors.

This book is intended to help women take what they already know as mothers and frame it in a way that helps them grow as managers. By providing a recognizable analogy, this book makes management easier. Working moms have enough to contend with. I want to give them an easy, quick means of enhancing their skill set.

I also hope this book helps women who do not yet have children to understand that motherhood does not have to be a career liability. In fact, I believe, as do most of the women I interviewed, that motherhood teaches us immeasurable lessons about being a good corporate leader.

I am the chief marketing officer for a Seattle credit union. Yes, I am a banker. I'm not an author. I'm not a business coach. I'm just a gal with three kids and lots of impressive friends. I do have a notable track record of growing business—two of the business lines I have overseen doubled and tripled under my leadership. I have employees who have followed me from one company to another. I have people who have worked for and with me for over a decade. My company has won many best-places-to-work awards. And most notably, my company continues to be profitable in a time when many of the largest financial institutions are failing.

There is no doubt that the coming years will be challenging for our country and for all of us earning a living in business. That makes it even more crucial that we lead with dignity. We must shape our spheres of influence in ways that create prosperity—for those we supervise and for the companies we serve.

The ideas in this book are not complex. They are simple and straightforward. I hope you'll laugh a little, learn a little, and walk away a better boss.

01

Getting Dressed Can Take All Morning

I tell my daughters, "We can do this the easy way, or we can do it the hard way." The first time I said this, my daughter would not sit still long enough for me to take off her clothes to put on her pajamas. She was not yet two and was determined to jump on the bed rather than get ready for it. I knew I was nearing that point where I would be forced to physically overpower her. Years later, I'm still amazed at how long getting ready for bed, for school, or for an outing can take.

It is human nature to resist that transition from one stage of the day (or life, or career) to the next. Whether we are six or sixty, we resist change.

The reasons we go to battle over transitions with our children are strikingly similar to the reasons we have trouble with our staff during times of change.

There are three important similarities between the parent/child and the manager/employee relationships during transitional periods. As parents and as managers,

- We are farther along in the process.
- We have a broader understanding of the greater need for the change.
- We have more control over our environment.

By the time my children are waking up in the morning, I have been up for at least two hours. I am showered. I've had my coffee. I've planned my day. I am ready to go. They are still rubbing their tired little eyes as I throw open their curtains and sing cheerily, "Let's go!" They don't have the motor skills yet to say, "Slow down. I need a moment to catch up with you." Instead, they pout or brood or ignore my impassioned pleas to hurry.

Our employee situation is no different. If you are the boss of other people, chances are, when a change happens, you have known about it for a longer period of time. You may have sat at the table where the decision to make the change was discussed and made. You have had time to adjust to the change. When you present the change to your staff, never forget that they are several steps behind you in the understanding and acceptance journey. Give them time to catch up with you and be sympathetic to the fact that they, like your children, may not be able to articulate their need to have you slow down.

In addition to being several steps ahead of your kids, you possess a better understanding of the bigger picture. You know why it is important for everyone to be dressed and out the door by seven. What does your two-year-old care about being late for work? Similarly, when you are in management, you often see the broader implications more clearly than those people who report to you. When presented with a change, they may not be able to see past the fact that the change makes their job harder, or more uncomfortable, or less important. You, however, see how the change may save your company a great deal of money, give you a competitive advantage, or improve the overall quality of your organization. In a perfect world, sharing with your employees the strategic reason for the change should be enough. But just like with our kids, sometimes it isn't. When that is the case, figure out a way to make it personally positive.

Nancy Baker, director of education for the National Foundation for Celiac Awareness and the author of the book *Globally Gluten Free,* is no stranger to change. She has moved her family of five several times, not just from house to house but from country to country. She shared her secret. "I do two things. First, I establish transitional objects. When the kids were little, it was their favorite blankets. No matter where we were or what we were doing, they had their blankets. It was something from the past that comforted them."

Companies can have transitional objects as well. When I went through my first companywide reorganization as an executive, a wise mentor told me to pay close attention to employees' desks. He advised me, "We will go to great pains to explain the reasons for the reorganization and how it will benefit the company and all that, but while we are talking, every employee will be wondering where they will sit."

Without exception, in every reorganization I have ever facilitated, one of the first questions employees ask is, "Where will I sit?" So often, companies spend considerable time communicating organizational changes yet fail to take into consideration employees' desks. Desk space seems to be a nonstrategic item and therefore often overlooked. But just like the blankets for Nancy's children, desks offer a transitional object—something an employee can hold on to during times of change. When guiding your employees through change, make sure to keep a close eye on those things that are staying the same and mention them often.

Keep in mind that, as the person of authority, you have more control over the situation than others do. Truth be told, if you didn't want to get up in the morning, you could call in sick for the whole family. Your child does not have that option. It is human nature to want to control one's environment, particularly during times of uncertainty. Kids will test their ability to exert control through all sorts of ways familiar to parents. Perhaps it's refusing to wear the outfit you picked out for them, or dragging their feet when you urge them to hurry, or insisting on waffles when you give them cereal.

Do give people some control over the situation. Rebekah went through a stage where she insisted on wearing two different shoes—one sneaker and one patent leather. While my mother found this to be unacceptable, I viewed it as a way for her to let her creativity shine, and for her to have a small win in the daily getting-dressed battle. I figured she had her whole life to wear matching shoes, so I let her go crazy. Just because I would never go out in different shoes—at least, not on purpose—doesn't mean my daughter shouldn't. There are times when my employees handle things in a way that I would not. I try to let them exercise as much control over their environment as possible. This is especially helpful in times of change. While this is easier said than done, in both parenting and managing, it can produce far better results.

Darcy Kooiker, principal and director at Berntson Porter & Company, tells of a time when her former company went through a major building remodel. "It was hard on all of us." She laughs. "But we each got to pick the color that our office was going to be painted. We all got four color samples, and it was exciting. Everybody had some bit of choice and everybody had something to look forward to when the project was done. That is what I do with my kids. Every night before bed, we pick out the clothes they are going to wear the next day. They get to pick their outfit (within reason!). It makes things go a lot smoother in the morning. I also try to take that time to get them excited about school the next day. I think those kinds of things work because they give people choices and some control."

By understanding those three key points, there are a few things we can do to make change easier on those we must guide through the process.

First, be sensitive to the fact that change is hardest when it is perceived that something is being lost or taken away.

My teammate, Laurel, was responsible for alerting all of us when our Internet banking system went down. She would compose and send all-staff e-mails with updates.

After a while, the executive team decided that the number of all-staff e-mails we sent regarding various systems outages was excessive. They were distracting everyone when only a handful of employees needed the information. Instead, we decided to post system disruptions on the intranet. Of course, this decision was only one part of a larger discussion about boosting the staff's confidence in our corporation. The discussion spanned a few meetings before action items were assigned. It did not occur to me when I talked to Laurel about the change that she might question it. Since I had been working on it for several days, I was farther along in the acceptance process. I mistakenly expected Laurel to catch up with me with only a short explanation. In addition, I figured Laurel should see the bigger implications as readily as I could (like I sometimes expect my daughters to understand what it means to be late for work). But she wasn't at the table when we talked about how the weekly who-has-left-the-employ-of-the-company e-mail affects morale or how the all-staff e-mails about the elevator being broken in one building or the ATM being down at one site shake confidence in our overall corporate abilities.

For years, Laurel had been the Paul Revere of Internet banking in our organization. It was one of her major responsibilities and her way of connecting with the staff. I failed to consider what taking this away might mean to her.

When I first mentioned it in an offhanded way, her reaction was not the apathetic shoulder shrug I was expecting. The change upset her. So I went back to the drawing board and approached the issue with new sensitivity.

We tackled the issue in a two-part discussion. I reintroduced the idea, emphasizing all of the reasons behind it. I let her mull it over, and then the next day we walked through her questions together. It took a while before she could accurately articulate that it felt like some of her importance was being diminished. Laurel is an extremely competent professional and recognized those feelings for what they were—emotionally based reactions to a change that was made with no input from her. Thankfully, after a quick period of readjustment, Laurel was back to providing the helpful information she always had, only now it was on the corporate intranet rather than an all-staff e-mail.

Second, people want to know what to expect.

Tammy Gallegos, vice president of service quality at America First Credit Union in Utah, talks about one of her twin sons who has high-functioning autism. "When he was about seven years old, he really wanted to play football," she explains. "Playing football would be something that was new, and change is very hard for him. Although he wanted to play, he was afraid of being tackled or hit by another player. He was literally shaking the first time he stepped on the field. I felt so bad for him! But after his first tackle, he stood up and said, 'That wasn't so bad!' After that, he knew what to expect and he loved it. People just want to be prepared for what is coming at them. I think it is easier to overcome their fears if they know what to expect."

When guiding employees through change, communicate with them as often as possible. A vice president of HR once told me, "Just when you think you have overcommunicated something, say it one more time and then you are probably good."

Another good strategy is to make sure there is something to look forward to, something to focus on after the change is complete. During Nancy Baker's last move to Spain, she promised all three of her children new bikes once they were settled. When things got too harried or the kids got anxious, she would ask questions like, "Do you think you want a basket on your bike, or no basket?"

Once, a nonprofit agency I was working for went through an accreditation process that required a great deal of organizational change. The change team agreed we were going to a nice expensive dinner when it was all done. We did the same thing as Nancy. When stress mounted, one of us would pipe in with, "I'm going to have lobster. Yep. Lobster for an appetizer and crème brûlée for dessert," and then we would all chime in with our opinions of the best desserts. It was a way to relieve the tension for a moment and remind ourselves there was a light at the end of the tunnel.

Parents also understand the need to stay focused if we are going to facilitate change. We would not dream of walking into our two-year-old's room in the morning, saying, "I'll be back in thirty minutes. Please be dressed, with hair combed and teeth brushed before I return." Well, we may dream of it, but we know it will never work. We know that, when dressing a one-, two-, or even three-year-old, a small distraction can abort the entire process. If the phone rings when you have shirt, pants, and socks on, there is a good chance that socks and shirt will be off again by the time you hang up. (I am the mother of a born streaker. I have literally turned my head for thirty seconds and my naked little darling has whisked past me, all of my morning's work in a pile near the door.)

We should also keep in mind that we cannot have a short meeting, send out an e-mail, or make a quick phone call and expect meaningful change to take place. To help our employees through change, we must provide significant focus on them and their activities. It is no different from dressing the little ones in the morning.

Last, whenever possible, personalize the process. In my household, we learned early on that if we told Rebekah getting ready was a race, she would dress quickly to be the winner. While she didn't care at all about us being late to things, even things she desperately wanted to do, she did care about her sister finishing before her. Turning dressing into a race was the golden ticket for us.

Top 3 Take-Aways

1. When facing change, communicate to your staff as early in the process as possible. Remember that they are a few steps behind you in the acceptance cycle, so give them a reasonable amount of time to adjust.

2. Devise a way to make the need for the change personal to your employees. While you may understand such things as the importance of meeting projected earning figures, some of your employees may not. When communicating the reason for change, speak in terms that all levels of the organization can relate to.

3. Whenever possible, give employees some control over the situation. If there is a major reorganization, consider letting employees choose their new titles. If the office is physically changing, consider letting employees select the color of their surrounding walls. Seek out and find those things for which employees can make a contribution to the change.

02

Rip the Band-Aid Off Fast

According to Paula Spencer in her hilarious book *Momfidence! An Oreo Never Killed Anybody and Other Secrets of Happier Parenting*, Band-Aids with cartoon characters or bright colors have been proved to heal boo-boos 50 percent faster. All three of my daughters confirm this fact.

One day, when Lexie was almost three, she walked up to me and quietly handed me a Scotch Tape dispenser.

"What is this for, honey?" I asked her.

She pointed to her three-day-old Dora the Explorer Band-Aid. The Band-Aid was hanging precariously onto her knee by the last remnants of dirty adhesive. The scratch that prompted the placement of the said Band-Aid had long healed.

"Oh, sweetie," I said, kneeling down to look at her lovely face. "Let me take that Band-Aid off. Your ow-wee is all gone."

She shook her head emphatically. "Put tape on it," she insisted.

"I know," I said in my best I've-got-an-idea voice, "let's take that one off and get a new one!"

"No, Mommy. Please? Please put tape on it."

When Lexie says "please" in that sweet little voice, I rarely can resist. I put tape on that dingy old Band-Aid.

The next day, when the tape had dog hairs and dust in it, I put a new piece of tape over it.

And so it went for several days, until Lexie had a leg thick with tape.

When it comes to taking off Band-Aids, there is just one way to do it—fast.

And sometimes, guiding employees through change is the same. Mary Kay Beeby began her career as a software engineer at Boeing in 1976. Anyone who lived in the Pacific Northwest during those decades remembers the fluctuations at the region's biggest employer.

Beeby, who now owns MK Consulting, says, "When I was at Boeing in the '70s and '80s, we used to joke that there wasn't actually enough space for everyone. As long as there was a reorganizaiton taking place, one department or another would be moving and then the company could fit everyone in. At any given time, somebody didn't have a desk." She became well versed in helping employees cope with the stages of organizational change.

It wasn't until her next job, with a California-based

publishing company, that she was forced to push people through change quickly. "The publishing house was bought by another company," she recalls, "and they gave us two months to close the Seattle office. I decided we were going to do it in one month and be done with it. People wanted to complain about this other company coming around and 'firing' us all. It just wasn't healthy. People needed to move on. They needed to look for other jobs. It was time to say, 'This is going to sting. Everyone hold on. Here we go!' and plow through it fast. In the end, people thanked me. It was what we all needed to do."

Kirsten Lowry of Nintendo of America sees similarities with the seasonal temporary employees they hire during the holidays.

> They are put through a weeklong, high-intensity training right before Christmas. The day after Christmas, they get put on the phones. Many of them are nervous about taking their first call. They ask for a coach or for someone to listen in with them. Because of the sheer volume of calls, sometimes we can't do that. We are just too busy to ease anyone into it.
>
> But it's funny, they come back after a day or two of answering calls and say this is the greatest job they've ever had. After all, the people they talk to are all thrilled to be playing their new game and everyone is in good spirits. We train them as best as we can, then basically push them off the high dive.

They think they aren't ready, but they are and they end up loving the calls.

Top 3 Take-Aways

1. Help your employees navigate through change using kind and supportive techniques.
2. Realize, however, sometimes change needs to happen quickly.
3. When change needs to happen quickly, deal with your staff firmly and fast.

o3

Be Happy to See Them

The first time I left my baby in a day care, I spent my morning commute sobbing. The second day I dropped my baby off at day care, I spent my morning commute sobbing and my lunch hour searching the Internet for strategies for coping with one of the hardest things working mothers face—leaving your child in the care of another person.

I found a great piece of advice: Your daily day-care pickup should be a special time for your children. Focus on them exclusively and be visibly happy to see them when you walk through the door. At all of the day cares I have used, there is always a fair amount of distraction at pickup time—coats to gather, forms to sign, caregivers to check in with, a drawing I have to admire "right now," not to mention a horde of other children vying for attention. When I walk through the door, my focus immediately fixates on my daughter. I smile broadly and exclaim "*Ooohhhh!* I missed you today." She runs to me and I gather her in my arms, bury my head in her neck, and say, "Oh! You grew at school today!" Every day is the same ritual, and every day she laughs and hugs me back.

Victoria Colligan, founder of the immensely popular Ladies Who Launch network, says, "Since my office is in my home, I sometimes have to orchestrate complicated delaying tactics with my nanny. I'll have a three P.M. conference call so I'll tell her to drive around the block or keep the kids occupied. Sometimes I take calls hiding in the bathroom. Because if I see them, all I want to do is hug them, kiss them, and be with them."

This is the kind of motherly attention that makes kids feel valued, special, confident, and secure.

Okay, so picking up your coworkers probably isn't appropriate, but smiling broadly when they walk into your office can have long-lasting effects that you may never have imagined.

Like many managers, I am a far greater taskmaster than I am a people person. After the concept of this book came to me, I decided to perform a highly scientific experiment. I took this parenting concept (be happy to see them) and tested it at the office. I selected one group of people (the test group) and every time they walked into my office or I saw them in the hall, I smiled broadly at them and said hello and used their name. I basically went out of my way to be extra-nice to them. The second group (the control group), I interacted with just as I had every other day of the week.

One of my favorite quotes comes from Karen Casey:

"An idea as simple as gently smiling at everyone before even saying a word can make the day far more productive and peaceful, and far less dramatic." It certainly worked for me. I began to see my partnership with my test group strengthen. They began to look out for my best interests. They began to come to me with information to keep me more in the loop. They were more loyal to me when I was not in the room—a huge asset for any executive. They seemed simply to like me more. I realized after that experiment that I will never underestimate the value in being genuinely liked by employees.

The effect of a facial expression of acceptance can be equally profound in infants and adults.

Ruthann Howell, CEO and president of Family Services, describes the Still Face video they use in training young mothers on the importance of the simple act of reflective parenting.

> In the video, a baby is sitting in a high chair and the mom enters the room and you can see the baby light up. There is a voice-over describing how all of this is unfolding. The mother makes silly faces at the baby and the baby bounces and squeals with delight. Then the voice-over says, "Watch what happens when the mother becomes unresponsive." Suddenly, the mother's face goes completely void of expression. Within seconds, you can see the baby start to unravel. Within a minute, the baby is crying. When you are watching the video, it is almost

impossible not to say, "Respond to the baby!" The effects of nonresponsiveness are so evident.

Managing people is not dissimilar in this respect. People do better when you look them in the eye. People not only want to understand what you are thinking (which is easier to decipher when you give them ample physical cues), they also want to be assured that they are having a positive effect on you.

The ironic thing about this is that studies have shown that high levels of stress often make people skip affirming facial expressions. You can walk through what this might mean. You take an already stressful situation and make it more stressful by giving mixed—or worse, negative—facial cues. It compounds the problem, often without the people on either side of the interaction even realizing it.

But don't stop at greeting people with an open and friendly face. Go one step farther and give them your undivided attention. It is as important to your employees as it is to your kids.

"I'll do things that wouldn't make sense to other people," says Victoria Colligan, "like having the nanny pick up one daughter while I pick up the other. Maybe the nanny arranges a playdate for one so I can spend time with the other. I love giving my undivided attention to the girls whenever I can." This is the kind of face time that humans thrive on.

Finnish-born Kristiina Hiukka, owner and founder

of Big Agenda Coaching in Seattle, once had a professor in Finland who had a tremendous impact on her. "When I went to her office to discuss my project, she turned off her phone, shut her door, and focused all of her attention on me. I realized how powerful being a recipient of someone's undivided attention can be. No matter what age we are, we all have the need to feel that it is important we are around."

This became a guiding principle for Kristiina in her communication with others—children and adults.

Years later, Kristiina saw her professor, now the head of the university, again and told her the life lesson she had learned from her. The professor sighed and said, "Oh! I wish you could tell that to everyone I work with. So many people don't take the time to listen to others. Even at high-level negotiations, many allow themselves to be distracted by cell phones and e-mails and BlackBerrys as if the machines are more important than people these days. It is extremely rude and it shows poor judgment."

"KeyBank addresses this in our Key Cultural Training," explains Mickey Mencin, SVP of advertising. "We state it simply: Be here now. When you are talking with someone, focus on him. Listen to what he is saying. Not only does this make the other person feel validated, but it is also far more efficient. If you understand something the first time it is told to you, you make fewer mistakes, have to recheck things less often, and can just get things done faster. People think they are getting more done when they check e-mails while trying to meet with someone, but it isn't true. You get more done if you focus on the moment."

In her recent book, *Distracted: The Erosion of Attention and the Coming Dark Age*, Maggie Jackson examines how, day by day, our hypermobile, cybercentric, interrupt-driven lives erode our capacity for deep focus and awareness. Jackson clearly hit a nerve with her book. The immediate response was tremendous, including articles in *The Wall Street Journal, The New York Times*, and *Business Week*.

Jackson urges us to create a culture of attention, recover the ability to pause, focus, connect, judge, and enter deeply into a relationship or an idea, rather than slipping into numb days of diffusion and detachment.

Cathie Black, president of Hearst Magazines, puts it a different way in *Basic Black: The Essential Guide for Getting Ahead at Work (and in Life)*.

At its most basic, to compartmentalize means to focus on one thing at a time. It's an important skill for anyone to have, especially anyone who aspires to a leadership post. The tone of any department, organization or business is set at the top, and employees will respond in kind to how their executives lead. Any executive who is scattered and distracted will find her team responds in kind, so it pays to work on this skill.

How can you do that? Well, if you are in a meeting, don't sit there constantly checking your BlackBerry. Believe me, whatever it is can wait—and if it really can't, you probably shouldn't be in the meeting to begin with. When you're on the phone with someone, focus on what they are saying, not on responding to email or tidying up your desk. You might think that you save time by focusing on multiple tasks, but you'll probably just end up needing to ask the person on the other end of the line to repeat things, which just wastes more time.

But worse than wasting time, multitasking while talking with someone sends the message that that person is not important enough to get your undivided attention. As a mom, you see how your kids act out when they can't get your attention. At any age, feeling insignificant is demoralizing. Don't make your children or your employees feel that way. It isn't hard to stop what you are doing, look them in the eye, and really listen to them.

Top 3 Take-Aways

1. Remember to stop, look, and listen. When someone comes into your office, take your fingers off the keyboard, your eyes off your computer screen, and listen to what the person is saying.
2. Practice some exit strategies to deploy when a conversation starts to roll on too long:
   - "I'm working under deadline. I'm sure you understand. I need to get back to the project."
   - "It was so nice chatting with you. I'm running

off to a meeting so I have to go. Talk with you later."

Stand up and start to walk toward your door as you say these things.

3. Always remember that at any age, people just want to feel like it is important they are around. Treat them with this in mind.

04
Speak Their Language

I didn't really notice it until my in-laws came for a visit when Rebekah had just turned two. We were sitting at the breakfast table and Rebekah yelled from her high chair, "Bye-ba-bim PEEEEES." Without even looking up from the morning paper, I said, "She said *vitamin please*."

Later that day, my father-in-law called me from the living room floor. Rebekah was telling him something and he clearly wasn't getting it. She, of course, said it a little louder each time (an innate response to being misunderstood). By the time I got there, Bekah had her hands on either side of her grandfather's face and was inches from his nose shouting, "Dabe me gapa normdy." He looked at me helplessly. "She wants you to play the 'save me' game. Pick her up and save her from Normandy, the dog," I told him. "But the dog is sound asleep," he protested. "Doesn't matter to her," I said, and walked away.

When our children are two and three and four, we

devote so much time and energy into understanding them, encouraging them to communicate better, and cheering them for getting their points across. In the end, we are rewarded with family members who can ask nicely for a glass of milk.

There are three parts to communicating with two-year-olds. The first two are listening and interpreting. The third is speaking appropriately. Understanding a toddler can be like solving a forensic mystery. Not only must you determine what the word they are using sounds like, you must also fit it into the context of their lives.

For example, when my daughter says "wiss," I know she means "fish." That's an easy one because she often pops her lips like a fish when she uses the word. More challenging is when she says "help you, my." I know that she has taken a phrase I always use, "Can I help you?" and interpreted the words "help you" to mean "help," and she says "my" instead of "me." So "help you my" means "help me." Mystery solved.

Often, figuring out what our employees are trying to tell us requires just as much investigative study and deduction skills. They tell us things all the time without actually using the right words—or any words at all, for that matter. For example, one of my colleagues, who keeps a candy dish on her desk, removes it when she is angry with someone. Another one of my co-workers stops by my office on his daily run to Starbucks to pick up my drink order. On the days that he doesn't stop by, I know he is upset with me. The amount of time someone takes to return a phone call, a person's tone of voice when he or she discusses sensitive issues, and the defeated posture in a meeting are all signs of employees wanting to tell us something. Perhaps they lack the verbal skills to tell us, or perhaps they fear the consequences of speaking up and thus refrain from doing so.

Before I had Rebekah, my attitude toward this type of behavior was that if someone can't get the courage to come right out and say what is bothering her, then I don't have the time to address it.

With Rebekah, I realized what a basic human need it is to be understood—even if you don't have the words to communicate. Our daily trips home from day care sound like this:

> **Rebekah:** Tomma pooh pull-ups.
> **Me:** Thomas has Winnie the Pooh pull-ups?
> **Rebekah:** My like Tomma.
> **Me:** You like Thomas?
> **Rebekah:** Doh-wa funt.
> **Me:** The Dora picture goes in the front of your pull-up?

You get the picture. Should I ever not understand her, you can feel the tension mounting in the backseat.

> **Rebekah:** Wiley little ticket.
> **Me:** Riley is a little ticket?
> **Rebekah:** No, Mommy, Wiley little ticket.
> **Me:** Riley is a little tickler?

Rebekah: NO, Mommy, Wiley little ticket.

Me: Riley is with the little children?

Rebekah: NO, MOMMY, WILEY LITTLE TICKET.

God forbid I resort to the noncommittal "Uh-huh. That's right." She knows full well that I'm giving up trying to understand her, and she'll have none of it. That is usually when the screaming begins. I once figured out an hour after she said, "My want bent-ture, Mommy," that she had told me she wanted an adventure. Out of the blue, I exclaimed, "Oh! You want an adventure!" Her face lit up and she said, "My lub you Mommy."

Suzy Kellett, whose illustrious career has included stints at *People* and *Time* magazines as well as managing director of the Illinois Film Office and then the Washington State Film Office, recalls one woman she worked with. "The woman was talented, smart, and articulate but did not handle stress well. When things were not going well for her, she would take her long hair, wrap it up on the back of her head, and stick a pencil in it. Within seconds the harsh whisper, 'Hair's up, hair's up,' would reverberate through the office as staff would freeze in anticipation of an imminent blow, and it was never pretty."

When my timid and shy second child began to talk, the realization that being an introvert was not only acceptable but sometimes commendable overwhelmed me. Suddenly, all those years that I insisted my colleagues act with as much directness as I do glared in my memory as times when I was not fair to people different from me.

With little Lexie, I see how absolutely difficult confrontation can be for someone. I see how she would rather forgo her own happiness in order to please someone else and how things might upset her but she will put on a brave face because that is her nature.

In addition to lacking the verbal capacity to confront what is on their mind and to being adverse to conflict, employees may not be able articulate issues because they don't fully understand them. We see this in our children.

For example, Brenda Wilner, who retired from a successful career in real estate to raise her sons, remembers a new teacher at her son's school. "The teacher was really nice and enthusiastic, but he had this whistle. When he wanted the kids to do something, he would blow on the whistle to get their attention. The day after the teacher arrived, my son didn't want to go to school anymore. I kept trying to get him to tell me why. He said he liked the new teacher, he missed his friends and everything else; he just didn't want to go to school anymore. On a hunch, I called the school and asked the teacher if he could stop using the whistle. I convinced my son to visit school again with me. We were sitting on the side of the class watching, and my son looked up at me and said, 'He doesn't have a whistle?' Up until that moment, I don't think he could have even articulated what was making him uncomfortable at school. But seeing his relief, I knew right then my hunch was correct. It was such a great feeling—for both of us!"

There is an old Jewish proverb: A mother understands what a child does not say.

Lest you think this concept is only of moderate importance, consider the Cuban missile crisis. Robert McNamara, in the Academy Award–winning documentary *The Fog of War*, contends that it was President Kennedy's ability to understand Soviet leader Nikita S. Khrushchev that kept us from going to war. Even though Khrushchev never said it, Kennedy surmised that the Russian wanted to find a way to avert war without losing face. Based on this, Kennedy ignored the advice of his Joint Chiefs of Staff to bomb Cuba, and a nuclear war was avoided.

This has led me to a new philosophy when I notice that the candy jar is missing or I see my coworker headed off to Starbucks without my order. It is amazing what a simple "Is everything okay?" can do. Sometimes the response is generic: "Oh, I'm just frustrated with such and such project I am working on." And sometimes it is pointed: "I'm upset that you didn't go with my idea on this product design." But almost without exception, the acknowledgment that you sense something isn't right is enough to make people feel understood and therefore feel better.

Armed with this new insight, I started looking for clues when things were amiss among my staff. I was amazed at what I found. A certain employee's lip thins when she is upset. Another doesn't prepare for our weekly meeting when she is frustrated. The list goes on.

The desire to be understood is a fundamental human tendency.

Harvey Karp writes in his bestselling *The Happiest Toddler on the Block: How to Eliminate Tantrums and Raise a Patient, Respectful, and Cooperative One-to Four-Year-Old,* "The best communicators show that they truly understand someone's feelings before expecting that person to be able to hear their advice."

Linda Moy, who works for a major automotive manufacturing company, and her husband use the Happiest Toddler on the Block method with their young daughter.

> For example, if I take my car keys away from her and she starts to cry, I will get down to her level and say to her, 'I know you want the keys. It's fun playing with the keys. You wish you could play with the keys.' We basically repeat the word that is making her upset so that she knows we understand her.
>
> I have noticed that the same type of approach works in my office as well. One of the people who report to me is particularly concerned about doing a good job. I know it's important to them that they are contributing in a very real way every day. So when we have our check-ins, I always make sure to acknowledge their specific recent accomplishments. It's just an easy way for me to show that I understand them and keep our exchange more open.

In addition to honing our listening skills and hearing both what is said and what is expressed through actions, we must speak in ways that are appropriate to our child and not always natural to us. The most striking example of this is the high-pitched, repetitive, sing-songy voices mothers fall into when talking to their infants. Several studies that prove that this type of communication is not only pervasive in diverse cultures all over the world, there is some indication that this type of voice can also help adults learn a foreign language!

As our children get older we evolve the way we speak to them, but it might not match the conversational cadence and word selection we use with our friends until our children are well into their teens. When we become mothers, the range of our speech broadens. We speak differently to our baby, our six-year-old, our teenager, our coworkers, our friends, our parents.

At one of my interviews, a mother told the story of how her thirteen-year-old son answered his cell phone one day and she heard him dismissively tell the caller he couldn't talk and hung up. "My son is usually such a kind person. I couldn't believe how rude he was!" she confided. "When I asked him who it was, he told me the name of a girl in his class. I immediately said, 'You better watch it, mister! She is going to grow up to be a hottie and you'll want to hang out with her when she is a little older.' "

All of the women at the interview laughed, and one, whose oldest son was not yet four, said, "Or you could just tell him that he should be polite to all people, no matter who they are."

The mother of the teenager laughed and admitted, "I really do wish my sons could think at a higher level than that. But they're teens and it's all about girls. My goal is to get them to be decent, good people. Sometimes that means I have to frame things in a way I wouldn't normally to get my point across."

At a different interview, Tiffany Bengston, of Starbucks, reiterated that theme.

My son is a year away from getting his driver's license. Right now, he is so focused on being a teen and what things are going to be like when he can drive. He is starting to ask for certain freedoms, so I talk to him a lot about trust and responsibility. I tie almost everything back to what he's going to want to do when he can drive. Like, the other day, he was supposed to be home by four thirty for dinner and he was late and he didn't call. When he finally got home, I said, "When you do stuff like that, you are not showing me you can be responsible. And if you can't be responsible, you are not going to be able to go as many places when you can drive."

It sounds like I'm kind of threatening him, but really, that is where his mind is at right now. When I phrase things in that way, he just listens better.

Kari-Mae Miles, a social worker at a Seattle hospital, likens it to when she has to communicate with surgeons. "Surgeons and social workers sometimes speak a completely different language. It is hard for each to understand where the other is coming from. I realized this one time when, instead of starting a conversation with, 'I've got a challenge with Joe Smith,' I started by saying, 'Joe, Tuesday's below-the-knee left amputee, has a problem.' With that description, I immediately engaged the surgeon and had his attention. As a social worker, I focus on the person and don't feel comfortable referring to him by his procedure. As surgeons, I imagine they look at things from the opposite perspective."

My communication style varies depending on whom I am speaking with. I rarely engage in a conversation with my sales folks without asking how they are doing and talking a little bit about personal matters. When dealing with finance people, I like to have data available and to keep the conversation linear and concise. And then there's the up-and-coming under-twenty-five crowd. I am finding that, on the whole, this generation of workers expects justification for decisions, appreciates irreverence, and demands transparency.

Every person has a communication style that fits best with his or her personality. Whether it is friendly and chatty or professional and efficient, there is a communication type that is most effective for every person. Discover those styles and use them with the correct people.

Top 3 Take-Aways

1. Study how your teammates communicate with you when they are not using words. Learn the meanings behind their nonverbal language.
2. Be sensitive to these cues and use them to your advantage.
3. Understand what type of communication works best with your coworkers and engage them on those terms.

o5

*Never Underestimate the Power
of Kiss It Make It Better*

Moms know two things well. They know the power of kiss it make it better and they know their children's I'm-hurt-for-real cry.

When raising a toddler, seldom does a day go by without a boo-boo. Boo-boos come in all shapes and sizes—real and imaginary (lucky for us moms, most are fairly imaginary). Typical boo-boos go away with a kiss-it-make-it-better moment. It is your child's way of saying, "I need a little attention." Many employee complaints are the same. It is understandable for workers to want a little time with their supervisor to share the challenges they are facing with their jobs. These types of interactions usually call for a quick ear and a bit of empathy, and everyone goes away feeling a little better.

Then there are the boo-boos that require Band-Aids. If my daughters are any indication of the market, the Band-Aid business must be booming. Nothing turns a frown upside down like a Band-Aid. Band-Aids are reserved for those times when the boo-boo is a bit more than imaginary but not enough to break out the Neosporin.

When employees come into your office with "Band-Aid" problems, you need to be more creative. These types of complaints generally require some step toward resolution. Often the best approach is to talk through the problem and come to a shared conclusion on how the employee can solve the problem herself.

Jennifer Sussman, who has worked for both mid- and large-size companies all of her career, tells of a time when she dealt with a situation like this.

> I oversaw the design, content development, and user experience for our company's Web site. During a redesign of our site, my team restructured the navigation and eliminated drop-down menus. A few months later, a research firm made an offhand comment that drop-down menus were best practice for one of our distribution channels, and a few key leaders in our business asked us to change it back. The team was understandably upset. A lot of thinking and effort went into the original decision to change the navigation approach, and going back would require a lot of effort without any definite benefit.
>
> My team came to me very upset about the whole situation, so I went to our new VP and asked him if we could document and share our position more formally. Luckily, he said yes.

The team came together to document all of the things they had considered in the change. They provided strategic rationale, best-practice examples of other well-recognized Web sites that used their recommended method, and shared the benefits of their approach.

In the end, there were pros and cons to both navigation styles, and leadership decided that we should reinstate the drop-down functionality. The team was disappointed, but having the chance to explain their position made them feel better, and made it easier for them to move on.

If you don't have any influence, it is frustrating and discouraging. But if you don't have any influence *and* you don't have a voice, it's just plain demotivating.

Although the team didn't get to keep the recommended approach, they did get validation and appreciation for their effort and thinking. And that made all the difference.

The last type of boo-boo is the kind no parent ever wants to experience. You turn your back for one moment and hear the shriek, howl, or outright scream that is saved for serious occasions. These are the kind of injuries that require trips to the hospital, stitches, casts, or other unpleasantness.

Kristiina Hiukka tells about a time when her son was very young.

I never left him alone. Never! But one day I was so tired and I told him, "Mommy is going to lie down and rest for just a minute. You play quietly in your room."

There was not supposed to be anything dangerous in his room. I had checked and rechecked for anything hazardous a million times. I had just begun feeling relaxed on my bed when I heard a loud crash and a howl. I ran to his room and he was soaking wet with blood running down his face. It was horrible! He had wanted to look at his goldfish that was on the shelf. I didn't think he could reach it, but he had stood on a kid-sized stool and it was just high enough for him to get his fingers around the goldfish bowl. Of course, when he pulled down the bowl, it landed on his head.

My husband was out running errands at the time. I just went into autopilot and stayed calm, though inside I was terrified. I scooped him up, put him in the bathtub, and washed those little blue fishbowl rocks out of his head. I realized pretty quickly that he needed to have stitches, so in shock, instead of calling for an ambulance, I placed him in his car seat, piled towels on his bleeding head, and drove to the emergency room. My heart was pounding and my hands were sweating. Only when he was in surgery being stitched up and I got to talk to my husband did I begin to cry and tremble, letting fear come over me. It was horrible. But it was important to me that Markus never saw me freak out, only calm and caring.

Unfortunately, some problems are far less obvious than a fishbowl on the head. They creep stealthily into our lives with little warning—the lingering stomach-ache that won't go away, the delay in motor skills, the sense that something is just not right. These might not jolt you out of your skin, but they still require immediate, decisive action. These problems are more difficult because they are not so apparent. As a mother and a manager, you must be prepared to act.

I learned this lesson the hard way when the finance team putting together our annual budget asked me to increase our sales projections by 25 percent the following year. My strongest salesperson calmly explained to me why that projection was unreasonable. I didn't see it for the drop-everything complaint that it was. I took too long to address it. I didn't fight hard enough to lower that number. Several Fridays later, my strongest salesperson quietly packed up her desk and slipped a note under my door before she joined the competition across the street (literally). The two salespeople I hired to replace her did 30 percent *less* business the following year. I often wonder how that product line would be doing today if I had understood that the cry I was hearing was not the run-of-the-mill kiss-it-make-it-better variety but the true needs-attention-immediately type. I am certain had I done something at that time, I could have saved hundreds of thousands of dollars in assets for my company. Don't delay acting when your staff needs you to.

Top 3 Take-Aways

1. Recognize the difference between complaints that simply need empathy and a moment of validation and complaints that require you to act on them.
2. Don't confuse the two. If someone just wants to vent, don't try to solve his problems. Conversely, if someone needs an advocate, don't fail to act.
3. If your employee needs your support, don't put if off and don't be afraid. If an employee is worth keeping, she is worth going to bat for. That is your responsibility as the boss.

06

Hold the Line on Tantrums

Tantrums can brew anytime and anyplace. There does not need to be a logical explanation for a tantrum. Rebekah can ask for "kop" (rice crispy cereal) and change her mind to "teesa" (cheese) while I am pouring the milk, and she will explode into hysterics.

All baby books assure you that tantrums end about age four. I think the books are perpetuating these myths just so that you don't walk out on your child in aisle 14 of the hardware store when your little angel out of nowhere turns into twenty-nine pounds of raging anger that could give Linda Blair a run for her money.

Tantrums may become more sophisticated or more covert, but they never stop. All parents learn to minimize tantrums. We learn prevention. We learn cures for curbing one in progress. We learn how to keep ourselves from having one right along with them. The same techniques we use at home can be used with our staff.

First, be diligent about preventing tantrum-brewing conditions. There are a few key tantrum preventions that every parent knows. If your child is tired, hungry, stressed, or bored, the odds of a tantrum increase tremendously. This is no different with adults. If your staff is tired—they have been working long hours or too many weekends—watch out! If your staff is hungry—they are not getting the support they need or don't have the proper tools to do their job—watch out! If your department is in constant chaos or enduring stress, then be prepared to have tantrums. If you subject your staff to long meetings where you drone on or if they crave growth and you don't provide it, watch out. You are headed for tantrums.

Darcy Kooiker explains that she periodically makes her staff "go out and play." "I know they work hard and I know they are dedicated, so when the sun is shining and we aren't too busy, I tell people to get out of the office and enjoy themselves. That does a lot to relieve the tension in the office."

Michal Jacob is the chief financial officer at KCTS 9 Television in Seattle. "I worked on a project many years ago that was really stressful. A special team was pulled together and we were responsible for implementing a big change for the company. The team started to get stressed out and annoyed with one another. So one day, I said, 'Everyone, outside!' I had them all stand in a circle, facing inside, and I put something behind each of them. Then I instructed them all to turn around. Behind them was a can of Silly String.

They looked confused, so I said, 'Don't just stand there—get somebody!' It took a minute for folks to feel comfortable, but pretty soon they were all squirting each other and laughing and being goofy. I sensed that they needed to let off steam and it worked. Everyone went back to their desk a little less on edge."

With toddlers, it is easy to know how much they have slept or eaten. After all, you are the one putting them to bed and putting food on their trays. With adults, it isn't so easy. That is why it is important to check in often. If you do not have established regular meeting times with your direct reports, then set a reminder for yourself to check in periodically. Many of the women I talked to with staff larger than twenty say they check in biweekly or at least monthly.

Ask each of your staff, "How is it going?" and then really listen to their reply. Listen for clues of fatigue, stress, or boredom. If you see any of these signs, figure out how to deal with them so you can head off a potential tantrum.

Anne Kirk, an executive at the American Heart Association, tells the story of a former employee. "I would periodically glance over her calendar. I knew if I saw too much packed into any given week, I should give her a quick call. She was so smart and so talented, but she had the habit of overbooking herself. I learned early on that if she got spread too thin, inevitably she would snap. So if I ever noticed her calendar completely full, I would call and she and I would talk about the things that were 'critical, necessary, and nice.' I never told her what to eliminate, but the exercise of talking through her commitments helped her clarify for herself which of her things she could drop."

While tantrum prevention is key, every parent knows that no matter how well rested, well fed, calm, and occupied children might be, there is still the possibility that they will throw a tantrum. In these instances, the tantrums usually occur because they want something they cannot have.

Katie Drummond, an analyst at the American Institutes for Research in Washington, D.C., tells of how at the age of two, her son refused to put on his clothes.

My son went through this phase when he did not want to get out of his pajamas. We tried to reason with him. Ultimately, we ended up pinning him down with one leg and putting his clothes on. We would be wrestling him down and he would be bawling. Our day-care teacher told us we should just bring him to school in his pajamas. We had certainly seen other little boys show up in their Batman and Superman pajamas, but we didn't want to give in. We didn't want to set the stage for all of the battles in the years to come. We didn't want him to think that just because he doesn't like doing something that he doesn't have to do it. However, the fighting every morning did start to get to us and we didn't want it to continue every day. So finally, we let him put his pajamas back on over his pants, and when we got to school, we took them off. It seemed to work. He was fine with the layering idea and we had a fully dressed kid at school.

It is human nature to be upset when we do not get something we want, whether we're children or adults. Children's wishes tend to be simple—candy at dinnertime, to watch more TV, not to leave a friend's house. Adults' wishes are more complex—a promotion, a raise, their idea to be implemented, a parking space. But both boil down to a tantrum when a person's emotional response trumps his or her reasonable approach.

Drummond likens her son's tantrums to the people she manages. "Many of them are fresh from college and this is their first job. When things pop up, I'm not saying they throw tantrums, but I always keep in the back of my mind that I am setting the stage not just for my tenure with them but also for their entire careers. When I interact with them, I always have one eye on their future, much like what I do when I deal with my son. Tantrums are often the ultimate moment of truth. The way they get worked out teaches both children and employees how to deal with problems well into the future."

Luckily, when kids throw tantrums, you know right away what is going on. One minute they are fine; the next minute they are in the middle of the grocery store, arms pounding the tile, screams piercing the air. With adults, it may not be as apparent—a refusal to engage on a project, a snarky remark made at a meeting, additional sick days being logged. All are equally distracting and equally disturbing to innocent bystanders. And whether you are the mom or the boss, it is your responsibility to deal with it.

Just like with our children, it is sometimes tempting to give in to tantrums because it's the easiest thing to do. But just as we know that giving our kids candy before dinner or letting them stay up late is bad parenting, we know that giving in to our employees and coworkers is bad managing.

"When people get angry or annoyed with us, it's often for the purpose of getting us to do what they want," warns Lois Frankel in her book, *Nice Girls Don't Get the Corner Office*: *101 Unconscious Mistakes Women Make That Sabotage Their Careers,* "Don't fall for the ploy."

Suzy Kellett single-handedly raised quadruplets from the time they were ten months old while holding down a challenging job.

> When my kids were growing up, I would not allow them to make a fuss in a public place. I did not want the public to have to endure scenes by so many tiny-footed people. They knew if they made a fuss we would leave wherever we were. It took several trial runs of "fusses and departures" for the group to confront the offender with, "Don't act up or we won't eat!" I found if the kids knew what to expect, and what I expected of them ahead of time, I could take them to five-star restaurants when

they were very little and they would be very well behaved—all four of them.

When I started working in the film industry, I sometimes thought I was raising quads all over again when people in the business let their tempers flare. Once again, if I told production teams what to expect, it took the element of surprise out of certain situations. Otherwise, I would take them aside to get them under control. Just like with my kids, I would tell them to "settle down; this behavior is not acceptable here."

Don't underestimate what a change of scenery can do to a tantrum. If you are in the middle of a meeting, a simple, "Can I see you in the hallway?" can be quite powerful. If the tantrum has been the long, drawn-out kind, asking someone to meet you for coffee off-site often signifies the seriousness of the conversation.

The advent of e-mail has given rise to a new kind of temper tantrum—flame mail. There must be something comforting about sitting at one's computer screen. It certainly makes some people more courageous, or at least more risk tolerant. Throughout my career, I have had far more confrontational e-mails than face-to-face confrontations.

When you get e-mails like these, never, ever shoot an e-mail back in anger. If an e-mail makes you angry, read it, close it, and wait. If an e-mail makes you really angry, wait one business day to answer it or to decide an answer isn't necessary or desirable.

When I get e-mails that are confrontational in tone, I force myself to take them home and think the situation through. My preferred method of dealing with e-mail outbursts is to physically visit the person the next day. I love the look on someone's face when I walk up to her desk and say, "I'd like to talk with you about that e-mail you sent me yesterday."

While this approach, more often than not, startles people, it is often the best way to deal with hot issues. If you can tackle a problem in an evenhanded manner, the odds of you solving the issue increase greatly.

Never engage in e-mail tantrums. Tone is completely lost in e-mails. You might think you sound reasonable and friendly in attitude, but your reader may or may not hear your intended tone. More often than not, he will think you are attacking him.

When it comes to tantrums, know what is in your survival arsenal.

Top 3 Take-Aways

1. Check in on your staff often to make sure they aren't overworked or bored.
2. If you see signs of either, work quickly to determine how to minimize the problem.
3. If one of your staff does throw a tantrum, deploy the same tactics you use with your child—pull her away from the situation, speak to her firmly and quietly, and make it clear that kind of behavior is not acceptable.

07

Count to Three Before Giving a Time-Out

We have little trouble clearly telling our children our expectations and vividly describing the repercussions if they do not obey. We also understand that we must give them a fair warning before doling out punishment.

Parents who use the time-out method of discipline know the rules of engagement. Even if you don't have kids, you have surely heard the stern parent at the grocery store or restaurant who forcefully starts counting, "One, two . . ." If all goes as planned, the child modifies her behavior before the parent gets to three. If not, a time-out (or worse) follows.

In the office, however, we often shy away from the same sort of direct and concise communication. We let things fester, and by the time we address a problem, it has grown into an unruly mess. We let annoyances build up to something bigger than they necessarily need to be. Worse, the employee is clueless. When it comes to your expectations, do not be afraid to speak as firmly and clearly with your employees as you do with your children.

Heather Snavely, a public relations expert who has worked at Edelmann and Cranium, Inc., and is now at Microsoft, has worked with all sorts of creative and zany people. As a matter of fact, her job title at Cranium was head of the hive.

Each of us got to pick our own title. I was in charge of building buzz. So I took the title to the grand pooh-bah, the cofounder and CEO of Cranium. He loved my idea and so that was my official title for two and a half years.

At Cranium, our office walls were painted the same color as the colors on the game boards. If you looked at our office from a bird's-eye view, it would look just like a game board. We had yellow, green, red offices.

But even in that fun, untraditional environment, Heather still had to have some tough conversations.

When I went to Cranium, we were using Ketchum West as our public relations partner. After about three months, I realized I wasn't happy with the work they were doing. Now, there are a couple of ways a client can deal with that. They can start to treat you poorly because they are unhappy with you. They can stop using you as much as they should and start doing everything themselves. Or they can have a conversation with you.

I decided to sit down and have a conversation with them. I spelled it out very bluntly. I said, "I don't feel like you know my industry. I don't feel like your writing is strong, and you are lacking creativity. I'm not happy with the work you are doing right now. However, ultimately I want to be thrilled and I want to get to a point where if anyone ever asks me I say, 'Oh! Ketchum is the most awesome agency I've ever known. And by the way, if you work with them, you *must* request my team. If you can get my team to work on your business, you'll be golden.'"

On the agency side, there are a couple of ways you can take that kind of feedback. You can say, "Well, she is new, and she doesn't really know what she's talking about." Then you can disregard it. Or you do just enough to show you are making some effort.

But that isn't what they did. They actually listened. They gave me someone with toy experience who had worked on the Mattel team. They switched over a few things and made some substantial changes.

Within six months, I *loved* them. They were phenomenal. I still recommend them and I still look for ways to work with them.

Top 3 Take-Aways

1. When you notice a problem with an employee, say something before it grows into something bigger.
2. If you mention an issue and the employee does not change his behavior, talk with him again. This time, explain the consequences if the behavior doesn't change.
3. If you still do not get the desired behavior, make good on your word and follow through with the consequences.

08

Some Actions Require Swift and Sure Punishment

There are some actions and behaviors that require sure and swift punishment. Running out into a crowded street, for example, or trying to suffocate a younger sibling are things that we instantly recognize as bad, with no question in our mind, and we react almost before thinking.

My husband can describe, in great detail, the one and only time his father spanked him. For the 1970s his parents were quite progressive and didn't believe in striking a child. That was until Dave rode his Big Wheel into the middle of the street. "I didn't know what hit me! I was suddenly being pulled off my bike by the scruff of my neck and hauled into the house. I got three good thwacks on the bottom. I never, ever rode my Big Wheel into the street again."

Sheri Blumenthal, a first vice president at WaMu, tells of the time when her two young sons were playing near their boat.

My oldest son was always really good about wearing his life jacket when he was around boats, but one day he was playing with a friend near the docks. They didn't have life jackets on because they were playing on grass. They weren't paying attention and they started running out onto this dock. I was a little way up the hill, and I couldn't get to them quickly. I was calling my son's name and running after him and other people were calling his name. Finally, I caught him and he was fine, but I needed him to understand the danger of what just happened. I told him over and over, "You could fall in and you could drown," but he was still just kind of laughing. I realized he didn't understand the words I was using, so I said, "If you drown, you will never see me or Daddy or Grandpa Dick again." At that point, he started bawling. That thought clicked with him and he suddenly realized how serious it was. I might have pushed it too far, but I really needed him to understand the seriousness of running out on a dock without adults or a life jacket. It worked! He absolutely follows rules now. When we go on an airplane, he is the only five-year-old carefully studying the safety brochure.

Tiffany Bengston jokes, "I hear parents who wonder whether or not they should get their teen a cell phone. I tell you, if you ever need a reason to give your kid a cell phone, it is so you can take it away! Restricting this kind of privilege is the quickest way to get my son's attention. If I say I'm going to take away his cell phone, I've got his attention—*immediately*!"

A former colleague of mine in the technical field once had a second in command who blatantly undermined her. He was scheduled to help with a computer conversion over a weekend. On Friday night, he decided he was too tired, so he turned off his pager, unplugged his phone, and went to sleep until Sunday. Back to work on Monday, the computer conversion had failed and the company was in a mess. My colleague gathered her staff for a process assessment. In front of the entire staff, the man started to air his grievances with her management style, claiming that his poor judgment was actually her fault. His departure was immediate.

As mothers, we don't hesitate to reprimand our children quickly for things we know will lead to harm for them or others. We must have the courage to reprimand our employees with the same swiftness and forcefulness if we want to maintain a department free of harm.

Monica Ramsey, who has run her own company, worked for NPR, and is now with KCTS 9 Television in Seattle, showed up to our interview cutting quite a figure. At over six feet tall in heels, she sported a backpack and motorcycle helmet. As we chatted, she told me of a time when one of her employees started acting destructively toward the rest of the team. "Peer pressure is a strong force—even with adults. That old saying, 'If everyone was jumping off a bridge, would you?' The answer is often *yes*! I could see what was happening. This employee was causing the other employees to become more stressed and tense, and it was really disruptive. And you know, once that employee was gone, the whole team became more cohesive and far more happy. It really taught me a lesson about how one negative influence can affect everything."

Teresa Jones, a director for an international retailer, tells of an underage employee who was caught trying to purchase alcohol at one of their stores. The management team was divided on how to handle the situation. "We have always had an extremely employee-friendly corporate culture, and this was back when we were a young company. The employee was well liked by the other teammates and the store's manager was reluctant to fire him. Even though I liked this employee a lot, I was focusing on our liability, the possibility of losing our liquor license, as well as the message we would be sending to all employees if we said that breaking the law was acceptable."

That was almost fifteen years ago. Teresa is now a key player in her company's global-supply-chain management and spends a great deal of time working with the company's Asian market as well as traveling to stores around the globe. She does not regret the decision to dismiss that employee. "Managers have to make tough decisions like that."

Top 3 Take-Aways

1. Accept that sometimes in your career, employees are going to do things that are completely unacceptable.
2. Act quickly and with confidence. Usually, these instances require termination of employment. Keep your cool. Follow your company's procedures. But get it done.
3. No matter how difficult these types of situations can be, at the end of the day, you are protecting the rest of your employees, building a safe environment, and establishing yourself as a capable leader.

09

Don't Put Things in Your Mouth

We are consistently telling our children, "Don't put that in your mouth." We say it almost hourly when our babies are learning to crawl, but it doesn't end there. I remember my mother's mantra from my teen years: "I've spent thousands of dollars on orthodontia for you. Don't put that in your mouth."

We don't want our children putting any foreign objects in their mouths, but we are first to use our teeth when the aspirin bottle won't open. The habit that always perplexes me is putting nails or tacks in our mouth when hanging a picture. A hammer in one hand, a picture in the other, and nails in our mouth, our toddler watching with rapt attention. What is the last thing you would ever want to find in your child's mouth? A nail! Yet we set the example with nails, tacks, and pins.

As parents, we learn quickly that we are always onstage. Those big round eyes and kissable little ears are soaking up everything we do and say. Remember how shocking it was to hear your words come out of your toddler's mouth?

When Rebekah was three, she, my husband, and I stepped outside on a cold winter's day. From out of her sweet little mouth popped, "It's freakin' cold outside!" My husband looked at me, slightly amused, and said, "That one is on you!"

Jamie Chase, who founded and runs a strategic-planning consulting agency, tells a story of when her son emulated her.

When I was growing up, I was tall and gangly. I was labeled clumsy and so that is what I believed myself to be. I wanted to teach my son early in life that accidents happen and you are perfectly fine if you have an accident as long as you clean it up. I instilled that concept in him by reminding him of it when he tripped or spilled something. But more important, whenever I messed up, I would say it.

One evening, when he was about six years old, we were at a congressman's house, and I heard a big crash. It was my son. He had spilled something. As I was rushing over to him, I heard him tell the congressman's wife, in his little six-year-old voice, "Oh, accidents are fine as long as you clean them up." It was clear that the accident had not shaken his self-confidence as stuff like that did to me when I was young. I guess I succeeded in getting my message across!

We know that our actions must be congruent with what we are trying to teach our children. If I don't want my toddler saying "freakin'," then I need to keep that word out of my own vocabulary. If I want to raise self-confident children, I must act with self-confidence.

Since before Rebekah was born, I have been committed to raising daughters with a healthy body image. I have always struggled with my weight and I don't want my daughters to go through the same difficulty. I try to be on a diet. I try to go to the gym every morning. All of this I do without drawing any attention to it. My husband and I never say the word "diet." We talk only of healthy eating and good exercising.

One night when I was brushing my teeth, Rebekah came in and stepped on the scale.

"Thirty-five," she said proudly.

"That is a very good weight," I agreed with her.

"Mommy, you get on the scale."

"Me?" My heart panicked. "I'm busy."

"Why don't you want to get on the scale?" asked my uberobservant four-year-old.

Good question, I said to myself. This is the kind of thing she will take her cues from. I can't let on I am embarrassed about my weight. I am trying to be the role model for self-acceptance.

So I stepped on the scale.

"Wow! Mommy, you weight a lot!"

Great, I thought. Now what do I do? How do I turn this into a teachable moment?

"It's not too much." I shrugged. "Lots of grown-ups weigh the same as me."

"Mommy, is one hundred and [blankety blank] more or less than one million?"

"It's less, sweetie."

I acted completely unconcerned about the whole episode. But inside I was praying, "Please, baby Jesus, do not let her tell the neighbors how much I weigh, especially the mommy who is the young, blond, perky aerobics instructor."

It's a simple concept—we should model those behaviors we want to see in our children and avoid any actions we do not want our children imitating.

This is true at the office too. If we want our employees to behave a certain way, we must lead by example. If you want your employees to have a healthy work/life balance, don't work until eight P.M. every night. Conversely, if you want your team to go above and beyond, don't spend long lunch hours shopping. Don't speak poorly of other staff or departments if you want your staff to play well with others. If you want your staff to acknowledge their mistakes, you need to be the first to apologize when something goes wrong for which you are responsible.

Jill Vicente, who is raising dogs instead of children, talks about role modeling during a crisis. "I know I look to my boss to be that emotional constant, and I try to do the same with my employees. When they come to me with a problem and they are dealing with their emotional ups and downs, I say to myself, 'I'm not going to get on the roller coaster with them.' I need to stay grounded. One of the best ways to accomplish this is to show them how a leader reacts in stressful situations. They may be having a meltdown, but I can't."

Natasha Shulman, owner of Shulman Consulting, vividly remembers an early lesson her mother taught her about keeping your cool.

I was in fifth grade and had just moved to a new school and it was horrible. It was a hard transition and I wasn't making friends quickly. My eleventh birthday was in November and my parents let me invite four girls from my new class to a special birthday party. We were taking the ferry to Bainbridge Island for a fancy dinner, and my mom had given me this one-piece jumpsuit. I thought it was so beautiful and I was excited for the inaugural wearing.

While we are on the ferry, I had to use the restroom. After I finished, I realized that I had dropped the entire top part of the jumpsuit into the toilet. It was soaked! I tried to wring it out but nothing was working.

Finally, after about ten minutes, my mom came to check on me. She opened the stall door and saw me panicking. She just looked at me and said, "Come on, Natasha, this is no big deal."

She acted completely unfazed as she wrung out the top and stuck an entire role of ferryboat paper

towels next to my skin to keep me warm. Her calm-
ness made me feel secure, and a dramatic calamity
was avoided. I totally followed her lead. I keep that
lesson in the back of my mind as a business owner.
I know that I set the tone, and not just in times of
crisis.

One young, attractive, blond woman I interviewed had
the interesting position of supervising almost sixty
men and only a handful of women. She worked in the
typically male world of technology. "The guys will go
out after work for happy hour. They'll go have a beer
and play some pool. We go to Europe often as a team,
and lots of people go out to the pubs or go for big din-
ners after work when we are abroad. I tend not to go.
Not because I don't want to hang out with the guys or
that I necessarily disagree with going out drinking. It's
just that, when you reach the executive level, people
pay such close attention to what you do and what you
say. I'm very sensitive to the image I'm setting, particularly when we are on business trips."

When it comes to role modeling, Darcy Kooiker
suggests a clever twist to the idea of focusing on being
a good one. She recommends actively seeking your
own role models. When mentoring employees, she encourages them to choose someone to watch and then
imitate that person's traits. "Early in my career, when I
had little self-confidence," she confides, "I would picture myself as Princess Diana. When I walked into a
meeting, I would envision myself as graceful and poised

as she was. It helped me work up the courage to speak up." She tells her employees to pick out those things they admire in other people and then mimic them until they become habits.

I love the bumper sticker, "Lord, please let me be the person my dog thinks I am." Once I had children, my mantra became, "Lord, please help me be the person I want my children to be." The same can be said at the office. Be the person you want your staff to be.

Top 3 Take-Aways

1. Always remember that everything you do is being watched and imitated.
2. Think about how you want your employees to act and then act that way yourself.
3. Watch the people around you closely. If you discover someone with the strengths you desire, model your behavior after him or her.

IO

Read and Tell Lots of Stories

The American Academy of Pediatrics puts it clearly, "Read to your child every day." Howard Gardner, in his book *Leading Minds: An Anatomy of Leadership*, states, "Leaders achieve their effectiveness chiefly through the stories they relate." We read stories to our children because we want them to learn, because we want to bond with them, and because they like it. We tell stories to our staff and teammates for the same reasons.

Through the ages, great leaders have used storytelling to unite people and motivate groups. People learn and retain information best when it comes packaged in a story. Information doesn't move people. Stories do.

Amy Richards, cofounder of the Third Wave Foundation and Soapbox, coauthor of *Manifesta: Young Women, Feminism, and the Future* and *Grassroots: A Field Guide for Feminist Activism,* and author of *Opting In: Having a Child Without Losing Yourself,* knows a lot about telling stories. After all, she weaves her stories as well as the stories of countless other women into her projects in order to bring to life the very real challenges facing women in the twenty-first century.

"The interesting thing about using stories," observes Richards, "is that the power lies with the storyteller. No two people will ever perceive, remember, or translate any event in the same way. For example, I once had a woman write about me, and she described what I was wearing. She said I showed up for the interview in 'leggings and a sweatshirt.' But I am not the type of woman who wears leggings and a sweatshirt. When I asked her about it, she reminded me that I had just come in from a run. I was wearing running pants and a Patagonia jacket. In my mind, running pants and a jacket do not equal leggings and a sweatshirt. But you know what? It was her story and she told it like she saw it."

By verbally shaping an event—crafting what you say, what you leave out, what you emphasize, what you deemphasize—you start to build the framework for how your company will view the past. As the leader of any organization, you want to be the guide of that collective memory. It is that collective memory that builds the collective view of the future.

"One thing I see in well-working teams," explains Kristiina Hiukka, who coaches corporate teams, "is that they share stories. Stories connect people to their emotional side and have a bigger impact than just on an analytical level. Not only kids love a story; even large multinationals now use story strategizing as their corporate approach to building their vision, values, and mission. It helps teams work together more effectively and helps them bond."

Your stories do not have to be grand. They only need to be easy to understand.

"I like to tell my kids about the fun things I used to do with my siblings," says Paula Spencer, journalist and *Woman's Day* columnist. "I talk about the silly things we would do when we were washing dishes (by hand) or how we would fight over which of the three TV channels we could watch. It demonstrates to them that the fun things—and the not-so-fun things—they do with their siblings are going to be important to them for their entire lives. I like the idea of instilling family values through the stories we tell."

Those small yet significant stories are important at work. Again, they need not be intricate. As a matter of fact, Chip and Dan Heath, authors of *Made to Stick: Why Some Ideas Survive and Others Die,* suggest that the easier the story is to understand and remember, the more effective it will be as a motivator. Gather stories from your business that have the moral you want your employees to live by. For example, if you are in the service industry and you want your employees to provide exceptional customer service, tell them often of the time when an employee kept the store open a half hour late to help a harried customer or when a different employee helped a little old lady change a flat tire. Those are the things that corporate legends are built on. They are spirit enhancers. Have several ready, and tell them at every opportunity.

One of the stories I often tell to new staff is this. I was sitting in an airport one day and the woman in the seat across from me had a tote bag with our company name embroidered on it. I mentioned the bag to her and she said, "Isn't this nice?" I laughed and said that I worked for that company and I knew for a fact we must have screwed up royally for her to get that bag. Then I asked her what we had done. She answered, "You know, I can't remember now! The only thing I remember is I got this nice handwritten card and this bag in the mail after I complained about something. So many people ask me how I got this bag and I tell them about your company!" This is a great example of how often it is the way we handle our mistakes that turns average customers into loyal customers.

That story is short, interesting, and gets a point across in a real and personal way.

Most of us have heard the story of the super-customercentric store Nordstrom taking back a tire, when they in fact don't sell tires. The genesis and authenticity of this story have long been up for debate. But it is a great example of the power of a story.

Snopes.com, the leading authority on urban legends, sums it up nicely:

Legend: A determined shopper once recouped a refund for a tire from Nordstrom, a clothier that has never sold tires.

Origins: This is possibly the greatest consumer relations story of modern times—it's certainly

pointed to as such in a multitude of business articles. In this one simple vignette is captured the es-
sence of what it takes to build and maintain a loyal
client base: The customer is always right . . . even
when he's proveably wrong.

Nordstrom began in Seattle in 1901 as a shoe
store and grew into the largest independent shoe
chain in the United States. It was not until 1963
that Nordstrom expanded into the clothing market
to become the renowned nationwide fashion specialty chain it is today.

Nordstrom has become synonymous with customer service in a way no other chain of stores has,
with the "tire refund" legend doing its part to bolster that image. Nordstrom customers receive "thank
you" cards for shopping there. Unusual requests are
handled with aplomb by a knowledgeable sales
staff. Staffers have been known to hand-deliver
special orders to customers' homes or even to ob-
tain specialty merchandise from other stores for
customers who ask for those items. Those looking
to return merchandise are not challenged to produce sales slips or Nordstrom price tags for items
which are clearly Nordstrom stock. . . .

This story is so prevalent that it is part of American
pop culture. As Snopes.com further recounts:

In an episode of the television sitcom *Cybill*, when
Zoey asks about returning a dress Cybill snipped a

decorative feature from, Maryann replies, "Oh, pish. I've returned snow tires here."

Ask any Nordy (the name given to someone who works at Nordstrom) and he or she will confirm that the tire story epitomizes the expectations placed on all Nordstrom employees. Not only is the theme of that tale part of the Nordstrom corporate culture, it has permeated the perception customers have about the company.

Families, societies, cultures, and religions all use stories as the foundation of their shared history. Stories shape and mold how people feel about the entity and their role within it. Use stories to show your employees how you want them to act and how you want your customers to think of you.

Top 3 Take-Aways

1. Think about an event that has happened in the past that embodies the values you would like every employee in your company to embrace.
2. Turn that event into a personalized and interesting story. Practice telling the story.
3. Tell the story often. Tell the story to new hires, to customers, to the press, to anyone who gives you an opening to tell it. Tell the story over the years until people who have worked with you for a long time start to groan when you launch into it.

11

Keep a Memory Book

Experienced mothers warned me of this, but I thought it would never happen. I thought I would remember my children's milestones forever. Of course the day she crawled, the day she walked, the day she said "Mommy" for the first time would be etched in my memory forever. Two years later, I realized those mothers were right—memories fade.

Laura Fitton is no dimwit. Here is how Shel Israel, coauthor of *Naked Conversations: How Blogs Are Changing the Way Businesses Talk with Customers*, describes Laura: "Laura Fitton, founder & CEO of Pistachio Consulting, seems to be ubiquitous in social media these days. She sits on the best-attended panels at prestigious conferences and is surrounded by the most people when the talk ends. You see her name in traditional press being interviewed or in bylined content about social media. You see her in social media venues being asked her thoughts on just about everything."

I laughed when I saw Laura post this on her Twitter

site: "S (who came early) was 4ish/5ish something, Z I think 6 or 7? But, weird. I never expected to forget that so completely." She was, of course, talking about her two daughters, admitting that she could not remember what they weighed at birth.

I called her to talk about this. Our conversation was as lively as she is.

At thirty-three and a third weeks, I suddenly started peeing myself. I thought, Why am I peeing myself? Oh, wait! That's not pee! My water just broke.

My first baby was a preemie. She weighed four pounds eleven ounces. Those first days, when she was in the ICU, her weight was such a huge deal. We watched those ounces like they were the most important thing in the universe.

And three years later, I couldn't remember what she weighed at birth! Someone posted a photo of a newborn on her blog and I thought, Ooohhh, a baby, and I started thinking of my own daughters and suddenly it hit me! I couldn't remember what either of them weighed! For my oldest daughter, I found her birth announcement. But for my eighteen-month-old, I had to look at photos from the delivery room! I zoomed in on the little scale and could see six pounds thirteen ounces in the reflection in the mirror.

Life gangs up on you all at once. So much stuff piles up that you just forget these details. It must be a coping mechanism.

The same thing happens at work. How many times have you sat down to do an employee review and you can't remember the details? You know the employee has been doing a great job, but you can't think of one example to illustrate that. Just as you keep a memory book for your kids with important dates and descriptions, so should you keep one for your employees. Face it, our memories are short. By jotting down the good stuff and the bad stuff, over time you will have a much clearer and fairer portrait of your employees. It will assist you in your coaching. It can cover your bum in a lawsuit. And it will make review time a lot easier.

I keep an easy-to-access icon on my desktop. It takes just a few seconds to jot down my experiences. It looks like this:

Date	Employee	Incident
10/29/08	Steve P.	Dropped the ball on urgent mailing. Asked him several times for supplies and ultimately had to go to Lisa for assistance.
11/03/08	Leslie R.	Produced great *Times* ad in less than two hours and did it very graciously.

This memory list should not be only for your coworkers. Keep one for yourself as well. Every professional should have an updated résumé that is ready at a moment's notice. That is simply good career management. Along with this résumé, keep a list of your accomplishments, with as much quantifiable data as possible. Look it over occasionally. Not only will it make you feel better about yourself, it will be your secret weapon when the recruiter for your perfect job calls out of the blue. You'll be able to rattle off your talents without a stammer or a stutter. It will benefit you when you periodically negotiate a higher salary (something else you should do as good career management). It can also give you a good swift kick in the butt if you notice it's been a while since you've accomplished anything noteworthy.

This list should also include the mistakes you have made and what you have done to change your behavior. Woe to the manager who glides through life with a total lack of self-awareness. We've all worked with someone like that and understand how difficult it is to learn from someone who does not learn from herself. Protect yourself against this state by periodically forcing yourself to commit to paper your strengths *and* your weaknesses.

I advise my staff to keep similar lists for themselves. At review time, I ask my employees to complete their own review and hand it in before I start writing. Not only does this make my review easier by ensuring I don't forget anything, it also alerts me to any discrepancies in our perceptions *before* I am sitting in front of them, delivering the review.

Self-evaluation is not easy, but by completing it in occasional small notes it will be more comfortable and more beneficial over time.

Top 3 Take-Aways

1. Create an Excel spreadsheet with three columns: date, name of employee, and incident. Place the file on your computer desktop for easy access.

2. Whenever you or an employee does something good or bad, take three minutes to type it into the file. An example: "November 29, 2008—Brian Walker—dropped what he was doing to process a last-minute expense report for me and was so nice about it."

3. Every six months or so, go back and look at that list. Use it to compliment members of other teams, to do your annual reviews, or to check in on behavioral progress.

12

There's No Such Thing as a Family Secret

When I was a few months pregnant with Johanna, I had to pick up two of my vendors from the airport. They were spending a week at my credit union, so we had decided to have dinner together on their first night in Seattle.

As luck would have it, my child care fell through at the last minute and I had to take my daughters to dinner with me.

As three-year-old Rebekah warmed up to them, she began chatting.

"You know what?" she asked them. "One time Daddy ate Mommy's cookies what she keeps in her car for when her is hungry. Daddy took her car to ski patrol and he ate her cookies and she said, 'No, Daddy! You no eat my cookies! Only you eat *one* cookie and that's all.' And you know what? One time I threw up in the car, in a bowl! And Daddy couldn't go to the go-huskies game, cuz I threw up. And one time Mommy throwed up in the sink! She throwed up because she has a baby in her tummy and it makes her a little sick."

I didn't want my vendors knowing that I once barfed in my sink. I really didn't want them knowing that I have a stash of cookies in my car for when I get hungry. And I really, really didn't want them to know that I once yelled at my husband because he ate my stashed cookies.

But if you are a parent of a child who can speak, everything is fair game for the telling.

Jamie Chase, a single mom, tells of a time when she was trying to curb her family's spending. "My son was about four, and when he asked for things, I would tell him that he couldn't have them because we didn't have enough money. I thought I was doing a good thing by teaching him that you don't buy things when you don't have the resources. Well, that totally backfired. One night he and I were out with some friends of ours who are far more established and, frankly, just have a lot more money than I do. When the check came, they offered to pay for our dinner. I thanked them gracefully, and then my son burst out with, "That's good you are paying for dinner because my mom has *no money*!"

I was thinking how similar families are to corporations one day as I stopped by the little coffee shop by my house. As I was paying, a customer walked through the door and greeted the barista by saying, "Hey! You're still here!"

"Not for long. Tomorrow is my laaaaaast day," the woman making the coffee told the customer. "I'm leaving for 'better opportunities' as they called it in the announcement to staff. Everyone here is quitting. We hate it. Management *sucks*. Hopefully, if enough of us leave, they'll figure it out."

Once I wrote a post on our corporate blog about a finance company that was sending inaccurate letters to consumers, telling them their mortgage was under investigation. The first comments I received were from annoyed consumers. Soon, though, comment after comment came from employees at the finance company—some were former employees, many were current employees. All of the comments were about how dishonest and corrupt the company was. I didn't post any of the comments, but the traffic alone sent my otherwise inconspicuous blog to second ranking on Google for that company. Some of the comments detailed with great animosity how the president would stand up at company meetings and rail at the employees that separating homeowners from their equity was their number-one concern in life.

While these two examples seem extreme, they illustrate a good point: The way you act to and in front of your employees will eventually manifest itself to your customers and your community.

I'd like to think that I am a balanced, rational mother, wife, and boss. But I must admit that sometimes I snap at my employees with the same force and as little logic as I did at my husband when he ate my car cookies.

Luckily, my employees are more professional than the coffee-store barista and I don't make them as mad as the finance company made its employees. But I still can't expect to treat people badly and have them turn around and treat the customer with amazing customer service. I also can't expect to treat people badly and not have them talk about me on the Internet.

With the advent of blogging platforms and search engines, anyone is a journalist and anyone is an editor. If someone has something they want to say about you, there are no longer any gatekeepers to mass communication channels. A blogger can say it, and if she has enough readers, it will show up as the first listing in Google when someone searches for your company name.

There was an instance of this in the credit-union industry. A guy blogged about Vystar Credit Union. He was angry because they made a mistake on his car loan. His blog post was titled, "Vystar Credit Union is the Worst Bank Ever." On June 6, 2006, he wrote, "No matter what you might be thinking of doing, don't do business with the worst bank ever. I have many reasons for saying that they are the worst bank ever."

Unfortunately, for almost two years, when you Googled "Vystar Credit Union," his blog post was one of the top five entries.

Imagine if your company had paid for an ad in the yellow pages and someone purchased an ad right beside yours that said, "Don't go to this company. They suck!"

You would call the directory salesperson immediately and demand that something be done.

You should take action if the same thing happens on the Internet.

Here are a few quick tips for monitoring what is being said about you and your company on the Internet and how to respond.

1. Set your name and your company's name up for Google Alerts. This will send you an e-mail every time your name is published on the Internet. If you are a big company, you can pay to have this type of monitoring performed.

2. Periodically search your name. Type it in Google, Technorati, YouTube, MySpace, and Facebook. I also recommend using Summize.com (this will search Twitter).

3. Encourage your employees to bring Internet mentions of you or your company to your attention.

4. If someone writes something about you on his blog, check his site with a tool like Technorati. If the blog has a low relevance number, you can feel safe that few people know about or read the blog and you can let the comment go without response.

5. If someone writes something about you on her blog and the site has a high Technorati rating, handle it much like you would a traditional media reporter. If she writes something good, thank her. Make sure you do it on the blog. Bloggers love comments. If she has written something negative, contact her directly to try to work it out. You may also want to comment on her blog that you've heard what she wrote and you want to talk with her to solve the issue.

6. Understand and maximize your search-engine optimization. You want to have as much control as possible over your keywords (for example your name, your product, etc). If your site is optimized, it will be more likely to receive top ranking on search engines. There are plenty of books and many consultants who can help you with that.

One of the best strategies against an employee or former employee slandering you is to keep your house in order. Before doing anything at the office, ask yourself, "Would I care if this were written about on the Internet and it was the first thing you saw when you searched my name?" If it doesn't stand up to that test, you probably want to think twice before doing it or saying it.

Top 3 Take-Aways

1. Anything you say and do can be used against you in the court of public opinion.
2. Before you say anything, ask yourself, "Would I mind if this ended up on the front page of *The Wall Street Journal*?" If the answer is yes, think twice about saying it.
3. In the new world of social media, know what's being said about you and your company online. If you don't know how to track and respond to that kind of media, learn about it or hire a good PR company that does.

13

Appreciate the Dilemma of "You Said!"

I remember the first time I offhandedly said to one of my daughters, "We'll go for a walk after school," and then I got busy at work and I was running late when I picked her up. There was neither time nor energy for a walk. When I broke the news to her, my daughter started to pout and used that ageless argument, "But you said!"

"This was really problematic in my household," admits Katherine Ellison, author of the phenomenal book *The Mommy Brain: How Motherhood Makes You Smarter*.

My twelve-year-old son and I now have contracts. With all that I have going on, I sometimes don't have the best memory. So I'll tell my son that we can do something or that he can have something, and I'll promptly forget it.

He figured this out and so would sometimes tell me I said we would do something when I really didn't. He is quite clever. So now if I say I am going to do something, I write it in a contract and put it on the refrigerator. That way, I remember and he can't con me!

Writing down your commitments is a good idea at work as well. It's important to keep your promises and it's easier to keep them if you remember them.

I've got a notebook that I keep with me throughout my workday. During every meeting, every phone conversation, every impromptu e-mail exchange, I jot down any "action steps" I've volunteered myself for. At the end of the week, before I leave for the day on Friday, I flip through the pages of the notebook. The things with stars beside them are the things I said I would do. If I completed them, I draw a line through the task; if not, I note it for the following week.

This may sound a tad obsessive, but I honestly don't know how other people follow through on their commitments without some sort of similar system.

Management books of all types stress the importance of keeping your word, acting with integrity, and following through on your promises. These are all important principles for a manager. But it was not until I had a child that I fully realized the reason why. From the time we are old enough to recognize authority, we want the people in charge to *do what they say they will*. It's a simple concept. When you have a child, you learn quickly—don't say it unless you are going to do it. If you said you are going to do it, try your hardest to do it. And if you can't do it, be prepared for others to be disappointed in you.

One time the CFO of my company informed me that I still had several thousand dollars left in my conference budget. That day, I asked one of my staff if she wanted to attend a conference in San Diego in December.

As the words were coming out of my mouth, one thought was running through my head: Beware of the dilemma of you said . . .

Later that week, I was speaking to the CFO of the company about the conference I was sending my employee to and he grimaced. "Just because we have money, doesn't mean we have to spend it," he counseled me.

"But you said!" I wanted to pout. "You said I have control over my own budget. You said I could make the decisions as to who needs what training. You said."

I realized then that it isn't just that we want the people in charge to do what they say. It also stinks when expectations aren't met no matter what the situation.

My employee ended up going to the conference (my boss may be frugal, but he is fair). I walked away from the situation with a renewed conviction: Always do what you say you will. Simple.

Top 3 Take-Aways

1. Think carefully before telling an employee about an upcoming event. If whatever might happen is

potentially good, you will get someone's hopes up. If whatever might happen is potentially bad, you will cause someone to worry unnecessarily.

2. If you tell someone you are going to do something, write it down so you remember it. Then do it.

3. If you tell an employee about something and it doesn't come to fruition, be sensitive in the way you handle it. Even as adults, we do not like to have our expectations dashed.

14
Remember the Magic Word

I've never seen a study that calculates how many times a parent utters, "What's the magic word?" But I'm sure if a study were conducted, the results would prove it to be in the millions. From the time children mutter their first words, we are constantly reminding them, "Say please. Say thank you. Say you're sorry."

Jamie Chase talks about teaching her son how to ask for things nicely. "I'm a stickler about showing respect in my home. When my son asks for something and doesn't say 'please,' I either freeze in my tracks or start moving in really, really slow motion. My message to him is that people are more likely to help you, and more likely to help you quickly, if you ask for things by using a nice tone and saying please. I think that is so true in real life and in business."

When it was time to teach my children to use the terms *please* and *thank you,* I started noticing how many adults do not use those common niceties. Once I had my ears pricked up for the magic words, I was appalled at how seldom I actually heard them at my place of work. Worse yet, I was ashamed at how infrequently I uttered them.

We often get so focused on getting things done quickly that we forget to ask for something nicely and to say thank you when someone gives it to us. Not only should you lead by example, you should also be clear with your staff that you expect them to say please and thank you to customers, to vendors, to each other, to other departments, to the community at large. Nothing speaks louder than good manners.

Deborah Levinger of Microsoft, who runs some of the largest events for her division, says, "It is very important to treat all people with respect. I go out of my way to be sure that from the VPs to a small vendor to an admin, they all get treated with respect and get the credit that they deserve. For example, I gave an admin who had been working extremely hard on an event a new Zune music player partway through the process. This was a thank-you for her great work so far, but also I knew it would be something special for her hard work yet to come."

Saying thank you after a job well done is generally pretty easy. It gets a little trickier when it's showing general appreciation for performance over time. Sometimes it might be hard to think of appropriate ways to show your appreciation. Also, reaching out like that can sometimes be oddly embarrassing.

Elaine Chan is one impressive businesswoman. After earning a PhD in economics, she shocked the world of academia by choosing to work in commerce instead of at a university. She worked for several years at General Motors and at the World Bank. While working for these gigantic companies, she felt the pull of her entrepreneurial spirit. She left to pursue her next career in the world of personal finance. Along with being a wealth-management adviser at a major investment company, she is coauthoring the book *Chinese Ultra-Rich: What You Need to Know.*

Elaine tells of a rocky time for her professionally.

There was a lot of stress at the office and I was working long hours and coming home drained and on edge. My daughter, who was about eight or nine at the time, was watching all of this very closely.

Then one day, I sat down at my computer at home and there was this little box sitting there. It had a little bow on it and a piece of paper with a poem. It was from my daughter. I think she got the poem off the Internet or something, but it was so sweet. It read:

> *This is a very special gift*
> *That you can never see*
> *The reason it's so special is*
> *It's just for you from me*
>
> *Whenever you are lonely*
> *Or ever feeling blue*
> *You only have to hold this gift*

And know I'm hugging you
You never can un-wrap it

Please leave the ribbon tied
Just hold the box close to your heart
It's filled with hugs inside!

Oh! It made me feel so much better. I paused and thought about how innocent children are and how I need to keep this stress at work in perspective.

A few weeks later, a woman I work with was in a car accident. She was really having a rough time. I wanted to do something to tell her I was thinking of her, but I wasn't sure what.

I looked at that little box my daughter had given me and I thought, Should I? I mean, if I give something like that to a coworker, would she think I was silly?

Finally, I decided to do it. So I made a little box, put a bow on it, and copied the poem and gave it to her.

It meant a great deal to her and I was happy I did it.

I think sometimes we keep up these shields of professionalism. Doing little things like giving people small gifts somehow shows our vulnerability. That is often hard. We say, "I don't know, maybe I need to be a tough boss and a tough businesswoman."

But I say, we need to remind each other that the world is kind. We need to take the time to show each other that we appreciate one another, especially during the rough times.

Cathie Black advises job seekers to always follow up. "Always, always, always send a thank-you note or letter to follow up," she writes in her wonderful book, *Basic Black*. "It's a good idea to send thank-you notes at other times too, when you get a bonus or a promotion, or anytime you appreciate something your boss has done, either on the job or off. As a longtime executive I can tell you that all bosses love to get thank-you notes, and the higher up the ladder they are, the less likely they are to receive them. We're human, too, and a sincere note of thanks means a lot."

But perhaps one of the most conspicuously missing phrases in the professional arena is "I'm sorry." Businesspeople are often reluctant to mutter the two powerful words "I apologize."

I once got angry with another department in my company. I was holding a focus group of fifteen mothers from our community. I had set up the event weeks in advance and had told all the proper people about the evening visitors to our headquarters.

Just as the women started arriving, so did a team of painters. As the men in paint-splattered overalls started taping tarp to the floors, I asked them what they were doing.

"We are here to paint the room," they replied.

I was furious! I was embarrassed. I was uncertain of what to do. I was all things I don't like being.

For the rest of the evening and on through the night I steamed about the lack of communication of our facilities department. My steaming didn't cool down as I drove to work the next morning.

As I got out of my car in the parking garage, I ran into one of the facilities coordinators.

"Did you know about the painters coming in last night during my focus group?" I asked her.

"Oh, my God!" She put her hands up to her mouth. "I completely forgot! I am *so sorry!* I feel horrible."

Instantly, all of my anger dissipated. She had made a mistake. I get that. I make mistakes all the time. A straightforward apology and I wasn't mad anymore.

Mariann Carmen, a project manager at Premera Blue Cross, was once treated poorly by a boss.

> One of my projects was moved from Green to Yellow status, and in the world of project management that isn't seen as much of an accomplishment. Instead of having a constructive conversation with me, my boss chose to harass me about it and made comments like, "You don't need to focus on anything else when you have a project to pull out of the weeds" and "Did you get that project back to Green yet?" Both comments were made in front of my peers and he continued to berate me for the remainder of the week as if it was a new competitive sport on ESPN.
>
> Maybe things would have been better if I had told him I was sorry when my project was demoted.

I *know* I would have felt better if he had apologized for his lousy behavior afterward. It definitely was an example of mistakes being made and nobody clearing the air with acknowledgments of wrongdoing.

Authentic apologies go a long way in building the foundation of trust that is critical to any enduring professional relationship.

Top 3 Take-Aways

1. Always ask for things nicely. Often, tone is lost in e-mail. Think about making a request voice to voice so the recipient of your request can hear your intended tone.
2. Always say thank you when someone does a favor. Think of creative ways to thank people. Public recognition at staff meetings? Small gifts? Including others in the thank-you e-mails?
3. If you do something wrong, offer up a genuine and timely apology.

15

First Use Training Wheels, Then Take Them Off

During a crisis at work, we were in the middle of an all-hands-on-deck meeting when I noticed another manager becoming visibly annoyed with one of the people there.

After the meeting, I asked what was bothering her. She said she was frustrated that so-and-so did not come to the meeting with more answers and more recommendations.

That evening, as I was cutting up grapes for fifteen-month-old Lexie's dessert, my mind wandered back to the day. I thought about why my colleague had been so frustrated. But mostly, I thought about why I hadn't been. After all, I agreed with her. So-and-so was completely unprepared for our questions or to help us find any solutions. However, in the meeting, I defended and protected him.

One important thing to note about so-and-so is that he isn't a manager.

It occurred to me that a significant difference between my colleague and me is that I have children and she does not. I spend a greater part of my day making quick assessments about what my three daughters are and are not capable of. Can they navigate those stairs? Can she take her coat off by herself? Can she eat these grapes whole?

In turn, I spend a considerable amount of time doing those things for them that they cannot do for themselves.

Like the grapes. Many mothers of fifteen-month-old children do not have to cut grapes anymore. However, my darling Lexie had only two teeth at fifteen months. If Lex could, I am sure she would grow more teeth and neither of us would have had to sit through this grape cutting. But the fact of the matter was, she didn't have teeth and so I had to cut grapes for her.

And so it was at the meeting that day. I am sure, that if he could, so-and-so would have come to the meeting anticipating our questions with a plan in hand. But he doesn't have the skills to do that. That fact was clear to me—but not so clear to my colleague. Probably because my colleague doesn't have to exercise that thought process nearly as much as I do. Also, I have built up an incredibly high tolerance for doing for others what they cannot do for themselves.

There is a delicate balance there. As mothers, we need to recognize when it's time to let our kids do things on their own.

"Some mothers can't believe I let my five-year-old walk on New York City streets by himself," says Amy Richards. "Oh! I don't mean completely by himself! But when we are walking, I've got my younger son, so my older son may run ahead ten feet or so. I don't make him hold my hand like some mothers do. The fact is, we live in New York and he has to learn to walk down a New York sidewalk. He can't learn that if I hold his hand every minute."

With our kids, we know we need to eventually take off the training wheels, lest we risk raising the laughing-stock of the neighborhood. Eventually, kids need to ride their bikes without help. It will mean falling down. It will mean scraped knees and bruised elbows, but all that comes with the territory.

The same is true with our employees. The reasons we hesitate to let or encourage our employees to complete things on their own are many and varied. Perhaps it is because we feel guilty giving them more work. To which Lois Frankel says, "Don't let your employees delegate up!" Often it is easier and quicker for you to do it yourself; but Frankel says, "Resist that temptation—let them do it themselves." Perhaps you are afraid of their failure. Again, Frankel advises, "Let them learn to do it themselves."

First you must assess whether an employee is capable of doing a project on his own.

"It gets tricky," admits Sarah Rottenberg of Jump Associates, who manages teams on both sides of the country. "You can't just ask people where they stand.

If they're not capable, people don't know enough to tell you that they don't know what they're doing. And if they're just starting to get good at something, people will usually tell you that they're not very good, because they know how much they still need to learn. So I spend a considerable part of the first week or two of a project with a new team having long conversations with folks, figuring out where they are. I need to evaluate how much the project lead and team members can do on their own and how much I need to oversee, advise, and ultimately revise."

I find that sometimes the best—and frankly the only—way you can really know if someone is ready to do something on his own is to make him try it," says Kirsten Lowry. "During the Christmas season, we hire a large pool of temporary employees to help with the rush of calls we get. Since we don't have enough time to hold their hands like we do during other times of the year, we give them all the tools they need, we show them where to find all of the answers to all of the questions they might get asked, and then we put them on the phone. They get thrown into the fray a bit sooner than other employees. They are nervous before that first phone call, but after a few calls, they realize they don't need the crutch of a 'silent auditor' and that putting a customer on hold to ask a question is just fine. We often get better results from these employees than from employees who have gone through a more drawn-out process."

You must also assess someone's willingness to undertake a project.

Sandra Alberti, director of the Office of Math and Science Education for the New Jersey Department of Education, puts a finer point on that concept.

> Early in my career, when I was a teacher, I came to this phrase, "Can't or won't?"
>
> When I work with people and they are struggling and I talk to them about the struggles, I ask them, "You can't do it or you won't do it? Because if you can't do it, I'm cool with that. I'll help you." I feel strongly about supporting people along the way. But if people are just unwilling, I have little tolerance for that.
>
> It is the same with my children. I say to them, "You can't tie your shoes? Well, let me teach you how. What? You won't do it? Oh, now we have a problem!"

Just as it is important to determine whether an employee is incapable of doing something, it is also important to discern if she is simply unwilling to do something. Having an employee who can't do something is fixable. But having an employee who refuses to do something is a different story.

If you've got an employee who refuses to do something that needs to be done, you've got a problem on your hands. If it comes to that point, it is probably time to start discussing their goodness of fit within the organization.

Top 3 Take-Aways

1. Be diligent in your assessment of your team. Once you spot their limitations, provide them with the resources they need to learn and grow.
2. There will be certain things that some employees will never be able to do. Don't beat them or yourself up over these things. Figure out a different way to get them done.
3. If, however, a person is not willing to do the things you need done, he or she is in the wrong job.

16

Do Not Succumb to the Tyranny of the Tattletale

One day at work, I got a parking ticket. I parked in the CEO's spot and I was ticketed an hour later.

Let me provide some background. Our CEO is the only person at our company with a designated spot. The rest of us have a cutthroat battle every morning for the remaining spots.

When my boss (the CEO) was on jury duty, I parked in his spot. He has no problem with others parking in his spot when he is gone. In fact, he encourages it. I parked there, knowing he would not be in.

When I brought this up in my protest about the ticket, the head of parking said, "Someone reported you. I had to do something." Then he lamented over how many employees constantly turn each other in for parking violations.

So let me get this straight (I thought but did not say), every time someone reports a perceived parking violation, you hightail it down to the parking lot and put a huge yellow parking infraction notice on the offending car?

And you are wondering why we have a culture of parking watchdogs? I don't mean to be rude but, um, duh.

That is Parenting Survival 101: Never give in to the tyranny of tattletales.

I live with tattling all day.

It starts in the morning: "She got more cereal than me!"

It goes through the afternoon: "She won't share her toys with me!"

And on into the evening: "She hit me!"

And what do I do?

In the morning, I say, "You both got the same amount of cereal. Now pay attention to your own stuff and don't worry about your sister's stuff."

In the afternoon, I ignore it.

And through the evening, I tell them, "Work it out among yourselves, girls."

When I imagine a world where I give in to tattletales, I don't like what I see.

In the morning, the girls' cereal servings would be the size of Outback Steakhouse portions as I gave each one more until they all were satisfied they had not been shorted.

In the afternoon, they would never play together because they would be in one long, continuous time-out.

And in the evening the resentment of the afternoon

time-outs would result in even more hitting and fighting.

I wonder what our corporate culture would be like if instead of acting on every parking complaint, our head of parking said, "If the CEO doesn't care about his space when he is gone, then you shouldn't either."

Or ignored them.

Or (gasp) told complainers, "Talk to them yourself."

My guess is that far fewer employees would turn each other in.

Tiffany Bengston says, "My eleven-year-old daughter is fairly sensitive. My fifteen-year-old son, on the other hand, is kind of clueless when it comes to that stuff. He'll talk to his younger sister like he talks with his friends—with lots of put-downs and basic teenage guy stuff. It really hurts her feelings, though. So she'll come to me and tell me how sad she is. But instead of talking to my son, I always encourage her to talk to him. It is a way better way to teach him to be nice than hearing it from me."

Deborah Colby, VP of marketing at First Tech Credit Union, manages nine people under the age of twenty-five. "So when I say I manage kids, I'm not speaking figuratively!" she jokes about her office. "When my son started kindergarten, he would come home from school and complain that so-and-so did this or so-and-so did that. I would tell him, 'The only hands you are in control of are your own.' You can't control what others do, but you can control how you react to it. That is so true at the office. We get caught up in the petty things other people do that annoy us, and we don't accept the fact that when it comes to that kind of stuff, we need to start by first looking at ourselves."

Tracey Elfstrom, VP of communications at Qualstar Credit Union, tells of a time when one of her employees went to the CEO about an issue.

She witnessed something one of my peers had done. It wasn't a serious complaint that needed to go straight to the top, she was just chatting with him one day and she "mentioned" it. Of course, he took action and so my peer came to me, asking why my employee didn't just go talk to her directly. Suddenly, I found myself in the middle of a she-said, she-said drama. My peer asked if she could talk with my employee directly, to which I said of course. Well, they talked, and it didn't go well.

I decided to sit down and go over the situation with my employee. I coached her on how she could have handled things differently and how she could mend the current situation. When I was talking with her, she stopped me and said, "Why are you talking to me? What about her?"

At that point, it struck me how similar to motherhood this is. My kids come home all the time asking me why so-and-so gets to do such-and-such or telling me so-and-so did such-and-such bad thing. I always say, "I'm not their mother, I am your mother, and the only thing I care about is what you do."

I said basically the same thing to my employee. The reason we were talking about her performance is that as her supervisor it's my responsibility to develop and teach and guide her. It isn't my responsibility to do those things for my peer. I might try to influence my peer to see things our way, but when it comes to how the message was delivered, it's not my place to coach my peer. It is my place, however, to coach my employee.

Those two motherhood lessons are great lessons for the office. Worry less about what others are doing (or not doing) and worry more about what you are doing (or not doing). And, when your staff starts looking around the company and saying, 'They are doing this or they are not doing this, and that's not fair,' remind yourself that your job is to develop your own staff, not the staff of others.

Sam Reich-Dagnen, CEO and cofounder of the award-winning early learning series *Braincandy*, laughs about how people—young and old—want things always to be fair. "Life is never fair, especially with twins. That ripples through all of my children's interpersonal relationships with their friends. One of my daughter's best friends was not allowed to watch *High School Musical* (the kids were six) because her mom was concerned she would get the wrong message—you know, all that messy, catty, high school stuff. She mentioned it would be easier for her if my kids didn't watch it either. Well, guess what? My kids love *High School Musical*. They love the music. They identify with the 'good' characters and think less of the 'bad.' Overall I think they're getting the right message. And I'm not going to make them stop watching it!"

These types of issues come up all the time in corporate America. "Why does IT get to wear jeans every day?" Well, because they climb under desks and move around computers. You, on the other hand, serve the customer.

When my daughters ask things like, "Aiden got to leave school early today. Can I leave school early tomorrow?" I say no. They inevitably declare, "That's not fair!" I always say, "If life were fair, uncomfortable shoes would never be in style."

Still, tattletaling is tricky business. I know I am occasionally guilty of it. I sometimes find myself mentioning things to my boss simply because they annoy me. I forget that my boss happens to be the CEO and if he decides to do something about my complaints, that could lead to large ramifications for other people.

Sandra Alberti has a question she uses with her two daughters and her employees: "'Are you telling me this to get someone *in* trouble, or are you telling me this to keep someone *out* of trouble?' Little kids know pretty well when they are tattling. It gets more difficult when we are adults. But when you pose that question to someone, he knows right away if he is tattling or not."

Top 3 Take-Aways

1. Ask your employees, "Are you telling me this because you want empathy or because you want me to do something about it?" If they want empathy, listen and give encouragement.

2. If they want you to do something about it, ask yourself if this is something they could and should take care of themselves. If the answer is yes, don't get involved.

3. Resist the urge to make blanket policies to keep things "fair" among employees. You'll end up punishing those employees who don't deserve it and, most likely, not change the behavior of those employees who need it.

17

Be Nice to the Neighbor Kids

"I checked out her parents, I checked out her home, I watched her interact with my daughter, and then I said, 'No, this doesn't work for me.' " Alyssa Royse, an award-winning journalist and founder of Just Cause, describes a time when she didn't like one of her young daughter's friends. "Sometimes there are people who just aren't good for you. So I told my daughter, 'If you want to play with her, she can come over here.' I say no to sleepovers at her house. I try to limit their time together. But I am always nice to her."

Let's face it, there will be times when our children bring home people we don't care for. We know that it is important for us to be civil to them. It teaches our children the rules of engagement. Just because you don't like someone is no reason to be rude.

"When my daughter was fourteen, she played on a volleyball team with a group of sixteen-year-olds and she hated it," says Karen Thompson, director of sales and marketing at Triumph Expo and Events. "They were kind of mean to her and she was really uncomfortable. Some of it was in her head and some of it was real. I gave her the choice of quitting or sticking it out through the year. I wanted her to stick it out, so I talked to her about how playing with older girls would help improve her skills. She ended up staying with the team. It really taught her that sometimes you have to work with people you don't like and you just make yourself get along with them while you have to."

Being nice to your kids' friends also saves you from being the embarrassing mom.

Growing up in a small town in eastern Washington, I remember a crotchety old lady who lived on our street. Our street was overrun with kids, and whenever we got too close to her lawn on our bikes, she would step out on her porch and yell at us, "Get off my grass, you hillbillies!" (Growing up in the Northwest, it wasn't until I was well into my twenties that I figured out she was attacking my socioeconomic status.)

One summer day, her grandchildren came to visit her. They were sitting sheepishly on her porch, watching us play on the street. And then it happened. One of the neighbor boys hit a ball into her yard and she came out and served us the customary tirade. I looked at her two young grandchildren and thought how utterly mortified they looked.

As moms, we do all sorts of things that will embarrass our kids. Being mean to someone doesn't need to be one of them.

Last, if we pit ourselves against our children's

friends, they may very well choose the side of their friends. If our main objective is to raise safe, healthy, happy children, then we need to deftly guide them through situations like these, not draw lines in the sand and create unnecessary wars.

"You have to put a chapter in your book about being nice to vendors," an executive I met at a conference told me. "I work in an environment that is supernice, but for some reason, some people I work with think it's okay—and sometimes they even think it's expected of them—to be mean to vendors. I just don't get it. It harms our working relationship and it's embarrassing."

I thought about that for a moment. I actually had witnessed that phenomenon before. I had worked with people who were quite nice to our employees but could get downright vicious to vendors, particularly when on conference call. And my fellow banker was right. Time and time again, those vendors we didn't treat well didn't have our backs when we needed them most.

I floated this concept past a few of the women I interviewed.

"I am always nice to my kids' friends, as a rule," confirms Katrina Basic of iFLOOOR. "And since I work on the vendor side, I can tell you that being nice to us does matter! For example, we had one big client that did a 'vendor of the year' award. They would bring everyone to Texas and have this nice event and they would say lots of nice things about us and then, when it was done, the people who attended the event would come back and say, 'Whatever we have to do to be number one, do it for this company.' They would come back from these events so jazzed about being the number-one vendor that they would say, 'If we have to reticket all of our products for them, let's do it!' So yeah, I do think showing recognition and appreciation plays a huge role in vendor relationships."

Heather Snavely admits that she has been on the receiving end of a bad client/agency relationship. "We had one client who asked us to do so many things that were outside of the scope of our contract with her company. She actually wanted us to take care of her cat one time! She was the worst. We did a good job for her, of course, but we certainly didn't go the extra mile for her like we did for our other clients. Having been on the agency side, I can tell you that you will get a lot more from your agency if you are decent and reasonable."

Being good to people has far broader implications. It is the foundation for building a strong social network. And strong social networks are often the secret sauce to success, especially for entrepreneurs.

"I have never thought that I need only vendors. I try to think about everyone as strategic partners," explains Alyssa Royse. "I look for people who will benefit from a partnership with me as much as I will benefit from them. It's like the difference between a babysitter and a close friend. Yeah, it's good to have a babysitter, but what I really need is someone who I can call and say, 'My husband just cut his thumb off and I need someone to take my kid *now*!' In my company, I've partnered with people who know I've got their backs and they've got mine. Because of that, we can work together to share everything from content to technology to networks, and it makes all of us stronger, greater than the sum of our parts. Just like a community. I've built these networks around me and I'm utterly dependent on them. But it's mutually beneficial and because of that, it's sustainable."

"The key is to reach out to your network," explains Sam Reich-Dagnen.

My kids go to a really great, very diverse school. I know that if I am running late to pick them up, there are at least three people I can call and say, "Hey! Would you mind hanging with my kids on the playground? I'm stuck behind a train. I'll be there in a minute." And they'd do it in a heartbeat.

But the key is in making that effort and getting over the whole I'm-putting-someone-out idea. When my twins were first born, I didn't do that as much. I didn't ask for help and it was a mistake and it was lonely. As a matter of fact, I had a friend, who, after she had her second child, said to me, 'If I had known having two kids was that hard, I would have brought you dinner every night! Why didn't you tell me?!" It's amazing how powerful the mechanism can be when you put in a request for assistance, send out some smoke signals, raise the white flag, and your friends snap into action. I've seen it at my kids' school and I've seen it in my business— it really does take a village.

But as Lois Frankel advises, you must invest in building relationships. She astutely points out that the moment you need a relationship, it is too late to build one.

Patricia Cobe, cofounder of Mompreneurs® Online, knows firsthand how critical a thriving network is for a start-up business. "Our online community is a great example of how nurturing mothers can be in the business world. When it comes to business, they capitalize on the strengths they already have. They are patient, persistent, well-organized, but most of all, supportive. The women are great at building relationships, supporting each other, giving each other confidence. When you witness this in action, you really see how powerful it is."

Top 3 Take-Aways

1. Be good to people, especially those who do not work for you or for your company. Often, those are the people you need most in your career.
2. Nurture your social network.
3. Reach out to your network. By asking for help, you build stronger relationships.

18

Never Say, "I Told You So"

One day my CFO called to get clarification about my sales staff's commission structure. After I went over it with him, there was a long pause. Then he said, "Oh, I didn't know it worked that way. I didn't budget for it."

Now, to his credit, he did not say, "You never told me." But I could tell in his voice that he was frustrated.

Instead of my usual way of dealing with that sort of situation, which would have involved forwarding him the document I had previously sent him and reminding him that I had mentioned my concern about these commissions being overlooked, I tried a different tactic.

This time I said, with genuine empathy, "Oh, dear. Is there anything I can do to help?"

He sighed, said no, and that he would fix it.

Feeling good about my new approach, I decided to take it one step farther. In the past, I would have let this conversation bother me. I would have thrown up my hands and asked myself, "Does anyone ever listen to anything I say?" But instead, I said to myself, "Executives get told a lot of things. It's okay that he didn't remember." And then I let it go.

That night, as I was trying to get the girls to bed, Bekah, on cue, claimed starvation. As I poured her a small bowl of cereal, I said to her, "Come upstairs and eat that while I put Lexie in her pajamas."

It was as if my voice was completely turned off to her ears.

"Bekah," I repeated, "bring your bowl upstairs so I can put Lexie in her pajamas."

Still no response.

One more time. "Bekah, come upstairs with me."

Since I was making no progress, I started up the stairs.

I was two stairs from the top when I heard the shriek. "Mommy," she howled, "you left me downstairs alone!"

She came scurrying up the stairs, and I said, "I told you I was going upstairs." That made her cry even louder. At that moment I realized I had handled the situation with my CFO better today than I ever had before.

The only thing saying "I told you so" does is make you feel better and the other person feel worse.

Sure, it's tempting to think, Maybe next time they'll pay attention to me! as you put them in their place.

But let's be honest, three-year-olds always are—and always will be—hard to corral into bed and CFOs always are—and always will be—worried about foolishly overpaying employees.

I love to be right (and I hate to be wrong). But at the end of the day, what I really want is my kids in bed by eight and my staff compensated without controversy.

Telling people "I told you so" does nothing to help me accomplish those goals. If it means saying, "Oh, dear! Is there anything I can do to help?" instead of, "I don't know why it wasn't in the budget, I told you about it," then so be it. And if it means saying, "I'm so glad you came upstairs! What a good girl you are," well, then, so be that too.

While it might feel right in the moment to vindicate or justify myself, if I am to meet my long-term objectives, I must refrain. Instead, I will assist and praise and help others around me feel and be better.

I've also come to appreciate those people in my life who must try something for themselves. We see this all the time with our kids. Like the time someone gave my two small daughters bright pink feather boas. The girls loved them, but they shed like a mutt in spring (the boas, not the girls).

One day the baby picked up one of the discarded feathers and started to put it in her mouth.

I gave her a stern "No!" and she took it away from her lips with an annoyed look on her face. Again, pink feather up to the lips, another forceful "No!" and another annoyed look from the baby.

The third time she tried to put it in her mouth, I simply said, "Suit yourself."

The pink feather went in and the look . . . Oh, the look! She looked at me like, "Why in the *hell* did you let me put this feather in my mouth?! This is *disgusting*."

She spit it out with a look of sheer pissed-off-ness.

Isn't that how it works? You tell them not to do it and then the minute they do, they're mad at you for not stopping them.

Cathie Toone, project manager for Turner Construction, tells each of the people she manages, "Closeout starts on day one."

The process of closing out a construction project requires a lot of up-front work as well as work throughout the entire process. If you wait until the end of the project to take care of those things, closeout becomes long, painful, and expensive.

"Some of the people will listen to this advice and some just have to learn for themselves. It's like watching a train wreck sometimes," Cathie says.

We talked about how it's easier to manage employees who simply take your word for it.

"Yeah, those employees who have to see for themselves what happens when they touch the hot stove are challenging," she commiserated. "But I have to admit, those types do learn things better once they try it. They never make the same mistake twice."

Top 3 Take-Aways

1. Never say, "I told you so."
2. If someone tells you, "I told you so," let it go. She is just making herself feel better. No need for you to feel bad. In fact, try saying, "You did tell me so." You'd be surprised how easy it is.
3. Go easy on employees who occasionally do not take your advice. That's part of the learning and growing process and people need to go through it.

19
Don't Be Afraid to Say, "Because I Said So"

I have a special voice reserved for critical situations. I try not to pull it out at the grocery store or the mall. It is not the voice meant for keeping tired kids in line. It's the voice I use in the parking lot to keep them from dashing out in front of cars, at home when they start climbing up places that will kill them, or anyplace in the airport. It's my mommy-means-business voice.

When my two oldest girls were three and one, I had to take both of them on an airplane. As we were boarding, I needed Rebekah, the three-year-old, to get in front of me but I had no hands to guide her and I couldn't get her in my line of vision to make eye contact. So I turned on the voice. "Rebekah, stand in front of me and walk."

I noticed a woman in first class unbuckle her seat belt and start to stand up. I didn't give it much thought as Rebekah scuttled in front of me and we began walking down the isle.

We made a few steps and then the line stopped. I was a foot or two away from the woman in first class so I could hear her when she told the flight attendant, "My name is Rebecca, and when that woman said to get in front of her and start walking, she said it in such an authoritative voice that I was just about to do it! Thank goodness her daughter beat me to it!"

As moms, we know that every once in a while we have to act with complete authority; whether it's the tone we use or the words we say, there are times when nothing but a top-down approach will work.

Amy Richards knows this well.

Usually, I try to give my kids options or explain to them my reasoning behind a decision. "But sometimes, like the other night, my older son was playing with the Club—you know, that thing you hook to your steering wheel? So he was playing with it and then my two-year-old grabbed it. I took it away from him and he started crying and asking why he couldn't play with it. I started to tell him that he doesn't have the arm strength to control his movements when he's holding it and he'd probably end up smacking me in the head with it and I didn't feel like being smacked in the head with the Club.

But then I just stopped and said to myself, "Why am I reasoning with a two-year-old right now? Either way he's going to cry." So I just told him, "I'm the parent and I say you can't play with the Club."

In our roles as managers, we spend most of our time striving for collaboration and cooperation. We seek input and listen to feedback. We explain our motivations and incorporate empathy. But every once in a while as leaders, we need to simply say, "Do it."

I had a young employee who reported to a woman who reported to me. The manager gave me a heads-up that her employee was unhappy with the way we were structuring some of the commission payouts. He talked to her several times about it and when this failed to lead to any change in our structure, he asked for a meeting with me.

I listened to his argument. He wanted to take some of the leads from the busiest branch and disperse them to the less busy salespeople. I could see the host of problems this would present companywide and I didn't want to bother with it simply to enable him to make a few more bucks each month.

After he presented his piece, I said, kindly and firmly, "There are three reasons I don't think your plan will work." After I spelled out the reasons, he started to object. I cut him off. "You and I will never see eye to eye on this subject and a decision must be made and the matter must be put to rest. I understand your desire to make more commissions. That is fair. Let's explore different options that do not involve taking business away from other employees. I'm considering this discussion closed."

I took a cue from Darcy Kooiker (who used to imagine herself as Princess Diana to get through difficult meetings). I pictured myself as Cathie Black, president of Hearst Magazines. I remembered a passage in her book describing a time when her male counterparts disagreed with a female-only conference she facilitated. "I refused to waver. When one of them wouldn't let it go, I said, 'Look, let's agree to disagree, and move on.' And we did."

Channeling Cathie Black, I stood up and thanked him for coming and made it clear that the discussion was over. Finished. Anything either of us would have said after that point would have been a waste of time. We would never convince one another and, therefore, continuing to talk about it would be discouraging and fruitless.

Top 3 Take-Aways

1. It's usually best to achieve results through collaboration and authentic employee buy-in, but sometimes you just have to say, "This is the way it is and you need to do it."
2. Don't overdiscuss the topic. Put it to rest fast. Nobody benefits from hashing and rehashing a decision that has already been made.
3. If this feels uncomfortable, pretend you are someone else. I recommend Captain Picard from the Starship *Enterprise,* or read *Basic Black* and channel Cathie Black when you must be the strong boss lady.

20

Be the Good Mom

In *O, the Oprah Magazine,* Suzy Welch cited "trying to be the good mother" as a common mistake women in management make.

She defines "good mother" as the boss who tries to be everyone's friend.

While I agree that getting too cozy with your staff is a dangerous move, Welch has the definition of good mother wrong.

In high school, a friend's mom wanted to know all the details of her daughter's personal life. I remember them giggling together on the night she lost her virginity. Her mom reveled in being told everything.

Another mom bought us beer when we asked.

Still another mom helped us paint graffiti on a bridge one night.

None of those were my mother. I could not dream of having a mom like that.

No, my mom made it clear that she was not my friend. "You have plenty of friends," she told me. "You don't need any more friends. You need a mom." And she was right.

My mom didn't snicker about "getting to first base" or "going all the way" when it came to sex. She spoke to me like an adult and discussed safety and consequences.

My mom didn't supply me beer, but she made it clear it was safe to call her if I ever needed a ride home.

My mom didn't think vandalism was funny and she let us know, in no uncertain terms, that we best not break the law.

That is how a good mother acts.

Good bosses are the same. Good bosses can have fun with and care about their staff. They can talk casually with them and get to know them on a personal level, but at the end of the day, they must make the distinction between boss and friend.

A good boss is there to help employees succeed and grow and flourish. Sometimes that means difficult conversations, or unpopular choices, or unfriendlike decisions.

Often it means acting like a boss and not acting like a friend. Or acting like a good mother.

On this topic, Tracey Elfstrom says, "My staff has worked together for a long time and they have become quite good friends. As a matter of fact, they even take trips as friends. They went to Las Vegas together! They invited me to join them and I declined. I didn't say why. I didn't tell them I wouldn't touch that trip with a ten-foot pole! I don't want to know what went on. It wasn't until a few of the women became managers themselves that I told them the reason I didn't do these things with them. It isn't that I don't like them all a lot. I actually think I'd have a great time doing things socially with them, but I know it would make it hard to manage them if I crossed that line."

I vividly remember the moment I learned this lesson. At my first job out of college, I worked in a historically tight-knit group. My entire department met regularly for socializing. When I was promoted to management, I kept up with this tradition. I didn't see anything wrong with it until the day I had to deal with a performance issue.

When I spoke with my employee about her pending probation, she looked at me in astonishment and said, "You can't put me on probation! My husband and I helped you move last month. That is *not* how you treat someone who just moved all of your furniture across town!"

She was, of course, right. And I vowed at that moment not to put myself in that predicament again.

Keep in mind also that sometimes employees do not want you as a friend. It is often easier for employees to take coaching and decision making from someone who has the clear distinction of boss. Many years ago, my boss and mentor, Bill Hayes, remarked, "Being the boss is lonely." At the time that he said it, I didn't quite understand. Here is a man who is well liked by almost everyone who has ever worked for him and truly loved by some. His interaction with everyone is casual, friendly, and quite open.

But I came to see that he was rarely invited to the lunch outings and never to the after-work gatherings. It was certainly not because we don't admire him, respect him, or enjoy his company, it's just that, well . . . he is the boss.

I had to remind myself of this the first time I heard that someone on my staff was having a party one weekend. Several folks on my staff were going. When the party thrower realized I knew about the party, she immediately (if not a little awkwardly) invited me. "Ah, no." I smiled. "You are supposed to have parties without your boss there." And then Bill's words came back to me and I said to myself, "Being the boss is lonely."

I must admit, I sometimes have a small twinge in my heart when I see some of my staff going off to lunch together or when I know of happy hour gatherings that don't involve me. But I remind myself that just as my kids do not always want me around, my employees do not always want me around either. It is natural and the way it is supposed to be. Even the most beloved boss is rarely invited to social events.

Top 3 Take-Aways

1. Your job is not a popularity contest. Your first responsibility as a manager is to help your company

and your employees flourish. A mutual sense of comradeship between you and your staff is important, but it is not appropriate for you to become too intimate with your team. It is your duty to set and respect boundaries.

2. Do be caring, nurturing, friendly, and casual with your employees. You can be a good person without being their best friend.

3. When your staff meets for happy hour without you, chin up. That is the way it is supposed to be.

21

Make It Fun so It Will Get Done

Remember the movie *Groundhog Day*? Every day Bill Murray wakes up and it's the same day—and nothing *ever* changes.

That is what getting my kids into their pajamas feels like. It's a pain in the ass. Every night. And it *never* changes.

We've got the sticker chart. I read the books. I watch the nanny shows. I know these little stars beside "puts pajamas on" are supposed to motivate everyone to be good and get ready for bed. Sometimes it really works. And sometimes it doesn't.

One night, my husband stumbled upon something brilliant—the eeny-meeny-miney-moe game.

The girls love playing that game for eeeeeverything. So one night he lined up all three of them, started with one and tapped their heads in order, saying, "Eeny meeny miney moe, Bekah, Lexie, Baby Jo. My mother says to take off your socks."

The lucky girl tapped took off a sock, or took off a shirt, or put on a pajama pant, etc.

Now, every night, they want to play eeny meeny miney moe to get out of clothes and into pajamas. (Some readers might think this is a little too close to strip poker, but, whadya gonna do?)

Tracey Elfstrom admits that she has a similar type of game for getting her six- and five-year-olds ready for school.

I wish I could take credit for this one, but my son actually picked it up at a friend's house.

We line up at the door when they are all ready to go and I ask them questions.

"Do you have clean teeth?"

And they yell "check!"

"Do you have a snack in your backpack?"

"Check!"

"Do you have fast running feet for PE?"

Then they do a lap around the house.

There are several questions I always ask: "Do you have your thinking brain in your head?" and "Do you have your good manners?" I throw in a few new ones every day. When my son lost his first tooth, I asked, "Do you have a hole in your mouth?" I always end with "Do you have a hug for Mom?" It's fun and it gets them out the door on time.

One day I was sitting in a corporate meeting. We are talking about goal setting and front-line direction, and someone said, "What gets measured gets done."

The thought struck me. When did this become a fact? We all take this as being true, but is it?

When I observe my kids, I note this truism: What is fun gets done.

Have we strayed so far from what we were as children that we spend the greater part of our day working on what our bosses are measuring and mandating?

I argue with a resounding *no*.

I think we spend a greater part of our day working on the things we enjoy.

I've joked in the past that if we could get our staff to promote our checking accounts with as much gusto as they internally promote our holiday party (or annual coat drive, or quarterly blood drives), we would be bigger than Bank of America. So what should you do about this?

Meredith Weil, director of marketing, customer service, and Internet teams for Third Federal Savings and Loan, admits that one of the things that drew her to the company was their values: "love, trust, commitment to excellence, respect, and a little bit of fun."

It's the first company that I've worked for where all levels of management strive to work within the value system. The emphasis on the importance of fun and enjoying what you do has been so refreshing. I want to work someplace that works on having a little bit of fun. We [the management team] make fun a priority. As a matter of fact, next week we have take-your-child-to-work day, so we have all sorts of fun activities lined up. I have to admit that sometimes it feels like fun shouldn't be on the top of my to-do list. Like this week, I'm returning from a conference and I know I'll have a million e-mails to answer and a towering in-box, but I remind myself that this corporate culture is what brought me to the company and what brought others and makes us stay. Ironically, you don't have a corporate culture of fun and enjoyment unless you really work at it. So I'll go back to work and participate in the take-your-child-to-work program and answer my e-mails later.

The danger in events like this is that they ring hollow with employees if there isn't a fundamental satisfaction with the work they are doing. All of us have been in the situation where we hate our job—whether it's because of the bad boss, the unreasonable deadlines, or the lack of recognition. We arrive at the company picnic not wanting to be there and check our watches every few minutes. When our bad boss gets up and cracks a few bad jokes, laughing at him feels so disingenuous that it's almost painful to our soul. We go through the motions of the picnic because we know we need to, but the whole time we are wishing we could get back to our desks to get our work done or, more often, back to our families so we can forget all about the work we are forced to do eight hours every day.

Enjoyable working environments seldom create themselves. More likely, there are good managers actively guiding the corporate culture behind gratifying jobs. Here are a few things you can do to promote this type of workplace.

First, make sure that people are doing work that is gratifying to them, that they are not saddled with bosses who make their lives miserable, and that their basic needs are being met.

If you are not sure what an employee likes doing, ask! Some might not be able to articulate it at first, but push them to give it real thought. I do this periodically. Recently, one of my managers said to me, "I like working on projects that have start and end points. I get satisfaction from completing something, rather than maintaining an ongoing process. I also like working with my hands, making things."

We were able to design a few job duties that included projects that wrap up and go away when they were done. I also know that on the rare occasions when there are craftlike things to do, she is the one I should call on.

If there's something an employee loves doing and he is good at it, keep your mind open to the business possibilities. One of my personal interests has long been blogging and social media. In 2006, my company won Net.Bankers Innovator of the Year Award for the corporate blog I started in 2004. Invitations to speak soon followed. One day I approached my boss and said, "I think I can make the credit union some income on this thing." At first he said, "We are a financial institution, not a technical company or a marketing company." But true to his style, he let me try it. The next time I was asked to speak, I stated my speaker's fee. Speaking engagements and one-day consulting appointments soon had me earning more money for the company than some of our product lines. Additionally, my job satisfaction shot up. I was meeting new people, learning new things, and doing something that I truly loved—teaching.

But it didn't stop there. My dance card soon included a series of appearances at a networking program for women business owners. After hearing me speak, many of the women followed up with questions or called me for brainstorming. Eventually, some moved their business bank accounts over to my credit union.

It came full circle when my "hobby" started bringing in customers for one of our priority business lines. Not only was I earning income for our credit union, I was growing our core customer base in the word-of-mouth organic way that is advantageous over other types of growth strategies.

A great book on this topic is *First Break All the Rules: What the World's Greatest Managers Do Differently* by Marcus Buckingham and Curt Coffman. It sets a good foundation for the theory of helping employees do what they gravitate toward naturally. It highlights the success companies have experienced when they capitalize on people's talents and focus less on their weaknesses. If an amazing salesperson never fills out paperwork correctly, you can assign the paperwork to someone who is wired for such work and give the salesperson more time to do what she does best—bring in new business. This allows your salesperson to do what she loves and is good at. In turn, you stop wasting your time and energy trying to make her do something she will never do well.

It is remarkable the progress you make when you say, "Let's stop trying to pound this round peg into a square hole and start honing your natural talents."

Top 3 Take-Aways

1. Know what kinds of things your staff likes doing. When leading projects, match staff talents and inclinations with corresponding assignments.
2. If you are unsure what things your employees love doing, ask them. Work together on articulating it.
3. When you come across something that your employees love doing and it makes you money, take note! That is a powerful combination that should never be underestimated.

22

Have a Plan

Jill Heron, a business manager at Microsoft, explains that part of her success, both as a mother and a manager, is that she always has a plan—and most often an adjustable backup plan.

When I wake up on the weekend, one of the first things I ask my family is, "What's the plan?" Even if the plan is "lounging without a plan," I want to know so I can plan the rest of my day accordingly. I plan in modules that move around, both at work and at home. Dinner menus move depending on time, sporting events, and weather—flexible, like the day's activities when I plan for vacation with unexpected rain.

I'm the same at the office. I want to know what we are doing each week and month. I created a master team calendar with a dependable meeting and event cadence, and the team "syncs" to it. It even includes vacations and deadlines. My own calendar has blocks of work time that I can swap out if things come up. When the team aligns and syncs, there is less overlap, fewer conflicting meetings, and fewer last-minute deadlines.

I once worked with a man who was extremely smart, well educated, and seemingly talented, although there was something about him that always left me feeling a bit uncertain. It was only after I had worked with him for some time that I was able to pinpoint that thing that made him less effective than he should have been.

He never prepared.

He had enough intelligence that he could almost always wing it in meetings. But after a while it became clear to me that he never gave a project much thought between check-in meetings. Frankly, I don't think he gave our work much thought unless he was at work.

I imagine that most people who did not work closely with this man would not have picked up on this nuance. A few people who did work closely with him confided in me that they had a vague feeling that he simply wasn't a good manager.

Eventually, I came to the opinion that he did not manage purposefully.

I believe one of the main reasons he did not manage purposefully is he never forced himself to have a plan.

I imagine his day went a little something like this.

He would wake up in the morning, push snooze a few times on the alarm, finally roll out of bed, take a quick shower. On the way to work, he would think about his family and his hobbies and his next vacation.

He would step into the office, pick up *The Wall Street Journal* and a coffee, read the latest news. Then he would turn his attention to his e-mails. Read through those. Take a few phone calls, attend a few meetings, perhaps work on a few of his to-do items, have lunch, attend a few more meetings, and then leave for the day.

On his way home, he would think about his family and his hobbies and his next vacation.

You've probably worked with someone like this. There are a lot of people who fit this description.

Compare that to someone who manages purposefully.

She wakes up in the morning, quickly does an inventory of her day. What are the three main things she wants to accomplish both personally and professionally? She positions those in her head so that while she is showering and getting the kids ready for school, her subconscious is diligently working through the day's challenges.

As she drives into work, she mentally prepares her daily to-do list. A few ideas pop into her head and she takes note.

She arrives at the office, and before doing anything else she pulls out her calendar and scans the day and the week. She has set her priorities before she engages in the day-to-day activities of in-boxes, voice messages, and e-mail. How else can she determine if attending to correspondence is the most important thing she needs to be doing first thing in the morning?

She checks in with her staff on a regularly scheduled basis. They know she wants to be kept abreast of the most important things they are working on. She does the same with her boss. On any given day, she knows his critical initiatives.

When it is time to leave, she gets into her car and debriefs the day. She reminds herself of all of the things she accomplished, no matter how small, so that she does not feel overwhelmed as she leaves one world for another. After a few minutes of important self-talk about her working day, she changes her focus to her children. She mentally prepares for her next shift of the day. She walks through what they will have for dinner, what they will do for an evening activity, what they might need to do to prepare for tomorrow.

A manager who leads purposefully thinks about things before doing them or saying them.

So why aren't there a greater number of purposeful managers out there?

E-mail.

E-mail is one of the most seemingly innocuous items on our task list. Yet it is one of the most insidious enemies of effectiveness around. Resisting the urge to get "screen sucked" every morning is almost impossible. There is something about the *ping* and pop up of a message that makes the desire to attend to e-mails practically overwhelming.

But, as time-management guru Julie Morgenstern advises, don't check your e-mails first thing. E-mails are like a quicksand pit that can easily suck you in at the beginning of each day. It's easier to get the important things off your desk if you aren't trying to regain your footing from the e-mail quicksand.

I went fisticuffs with our management team on this one. At one time, our executive vice president recommended that everyone in the organization implement a four-hour e-mail rule: Each and every e-mail should be answered within four hours. My first reaction to this suggestion was disbelief. Why on earth would we want to chain ourselves to our desks like that? So much busywork gets done over e-mail and so much real work gets done face-to-face. I don't want to be a slave to e-mail.

I tell my staff that if something is so important it needs immediate attention, they should call me or come to my office. While I do understand my executive vice president's point that being nonresponsive to e-mails is rude and unprofessional, I also don't want to turn e-mail into the most effective means of communication by giving it highest priority above all other channels.

E-mail creates the great democratization of project management. Within my e-mail in-box, a message about the staff potluck sits alongside the announcement of a change in our strategic direction. The potluck e-mail is as important to the potluck organizer as the strategic-direction e-mail is to the CEO. Oddly, both elicit a reactionary impulse within me to answer—the potluck e-mail because it's quick and the strategic-direction e-mail because it is important. However, when I spend my day answering e-mails (which I think I could spend a better part of each day doing), I give up all control of my own agenda and work only on the agendas of others. And some people's agenda are far less important to me than my own.

It's not easy to be disciplined and focused on a plan, whether it's ignoring the nonessential e-mails, or taking the time to sync up with all the players on the team, or going over the plan in your mind's eye during your downtime. But this discipline is important, especially in stressful situations.

My company was going through a round of layoffs at the same time one-year-old Lexie needed ear surgery.

Lexie had been struggling with back-to-back ear infections. It seemed like we were constantly in the pediatrician's office and on one long continuous dose of antibiotics. Finally, at her one-year checkup, the doctor tested her verbal skills and determined she was falling behind, most likely due to hearing loss.

We knew that having her eardrums drained, performing a quick exploratory look at the condition of her inner ear, and putting tubes in her ears was fairly routine. We were a little embarrassed to admit it, but the thought of our little baby going into surgery had us worried. Neither of us slept much the night before in anticipation of our trip to the hospital the next day.

For prepping Lex, they put us in a little curtained-off area that had a few toys. The coordinating nurse explained the procedure to us. She showed the face mask to Lexie and put it on both me and Dave, then let her play with it. That was good. It got all of us comfortable with the method of anesthesia.

There were four people involved in the procedure and they came separately and introduced themselves. Each one explained the six steps for the day. (1) Lisa will come in and whisk Lex away to the operating room. (2) Carol will take us to the waiting room. (3) After twenty minutes, Dr. Anonsen will come tell us what she found. (4) After a few more minutes, the recovery nurse will come get us when Lex is regaining consciousness. (5) We will stay in the recovery room with her until everyone is certain she is ready to go home. (6) She will be very agitated and inconsolable. It is because of the anesthesia, not because she is in pain.

I am glad they told us four times. With the sleep deprivation and the nerves and the distractions, it was good to hear it more than once. I felt more in control because I knew exactly what to expect.

When Lisa came to take her away, the six steps went quickly into play. Lisa whisked her to the other room. Carol took us out and we waited for the doctor.

Then the recovery nurse came to get us. He warned us a fifth time about the confusion, agitation, and inconsolability. The moment he opened the door, I could hear Lexie crying. He walked us quickly down the corridor and they handed her to me. They sat me down in a big recliner and put a warmed blanket on us and pillows under my arms. It was the strangest thing. It was like she was a newborn again. "She's floppy," they warned me. And they were right.

When we got home, all three of us fell into a deep sound nap. When we woke up, there was blood from her ears on the pillow. I am glad they told me four times that that was normal. So it didn't freak me out.

When I returned to work the next day, I shared my experience with the executive team.

"You know," I said, "we've never done layoffs before and I know we are all a little nervous about it. It sounds silly, but it might be good if we said the plan out loud several times before execution."

The group thought it did sound pretty silly, but the CEO humored me and we tried it. Each morning, at our daily check-ins, a different person would quickly say out loud the eight steps we had for coordinating the companywide layoff in the coming week. We wanted to make sure we told the right people first and that we did it fast so that the rumor line didn't leave people sitting at their desks, drenched in worry and dread. We needed a representative from HR at every meeting and we wanted to give some folks the option of saying good-bye to all of their friends (there were a few people we thought needed to be escorted out quickly). Each department had meetings scheduled for different rooms in the building throughout the day. We wanted to tell them what was happening as quickly as possible. It was a complicated, choreographed corporate dance.

The day of the layoff was extremely stressful. Some

of the people who were let go had been with our company for many years. No matter how long you have been an executive, it is never easy to tell someone he is losing his livelihood.

But our plan for execution was carefully laid out and each of us had heard the plan and had actually said the plan aloud several times over the previous week. When it came time to implement, we were able to put our conscious minds to work and let our subconscious minds remind us of the day's flow.

Theresa Paccagnan, who has been a firefighter for eighteen years, contrasts her career with an episode in her family.

As a firefighter, we have all sorts of training. You name it, we get trained on it. We are trained every year on rope rescue, weapons of mass destruction, emergency medical training, just to name a few. We've gone over these things so much that when we get a call, say for a cardiac arrest, the team just goes into action. We do rescue breathing, apply and operate the Life Pac, perform CPR, all of it while barely speaking to each other. We've practiced it so much that it kind of just happens.

Once, however, when my son Nathan was little, my husband, Nathan, and I were out on a lake paddleboating. We all had our life jackets on and my son kept leaning out too far over the edge of the boat. My husband and I are both believers in natural consequences, so we warned him a few times not to lean over so far, but eventually he fell in. My husband and I looked at each other. We both had this look on our faces, like, "Well, are you going in to get him?" Since we hadn't discussed what we would do beforehand, there was that momentary pause. I ended up going into the lake to fish him out. It was June, and the water was really cold! Had I been on the job, we would have known who would do what under most circumstances.

Plans are important. In their book *Made to Stick,* brothers Chip and Dan Heath recommend following an example set by the army.

> The Army invests enormous energy in its planning, and its processes have been refined over many years. The system is a marvel of communication. [The army] invented a concept called Commander's Intent (CI). CI is a crisp, plain-talk statement that appears at the top of every order, specifying the plan's goal, the desired end-state of an operation.
>
> Colonel Kolditz says, "Over time we've come to understand more and more about what makes people successful in complex operations." He believes that plans are useful, in the sense that they are proof that *planning* has taken place.

While planning is important, it is really the *preparation* that is critical. My husband likens it to the times he and I have traveled. Twice we have gone on extended backpacking treks across Europe. Both times, he was responsible for the planning and preparation. There is no planning for the random taxi driver who picks you up in Poland and drops you off at the remote border of Slovakia with no instructions on how to get across. However, proper preparation will ensure that you know enough of Slovakian culture to know that hitching a ride with a passing local is probably safe and the only way you'll get to the bus station.

Just like the army realizes that the Commander's Intent is crucial, so do they realize that no battle plan survives first contact with the enemy.

Nope, life never goes according to plan.

As working mothers, we must accept and embrace this fact and refuse to let it beat us down. I start every day by listing the things I want to accomplish that day. I end every day by listing the things I accomplished that day. I remind myself that even the smallest things—paying a few bills, reading a new book with my daughters, listening to an employee work through a problem—are still accomplishments. Even the things that were not on my to-do list or the things that seemed least significant are important to someone.

Mary Kay Beeby has a similar habit.

I have five guiding principles that I determined were my measures of success when I left the corporate world and began consulting. (1) Work with people I like and respect. (2) Spend time with the people I love. (3) Have enough money to live comfortably.

(4) Do work that is meaningful and makes a difference. (5) Be physically fit well into my eighties.

At the end of each day, I mentally match my activities with these principles, feeling successful if I've fulfilled at least three. Defining those values and checking them daily has brought me to a place where I am happier than I've ever been.

While our to-do lists are endless and often overwhelming each day, we must remind ourselves that life does not go according to plan. Life is made of moments. We make a difference in countless lives small moment after small moment.

Top 3 Take-Aways

1. Manage purposefully. Give thought to your day, your week, your month. Be mindful of your employees' and your boss's projects and sync yourself with them.
2. When embarking on a stressful situation, say your plan verbally to commit it to your subconscious.
3. Life never goes according to plan. Don't beat yourself up over it. Celebrate what you accomplish and let go of what you do not.

23

Don't Mess with Momentum

One day I got mad at my husband.

We had afternoon family plans and we were on our way out the door. Coats were on. The potty-trained one had gone to the bathroom. The baby was strapped in the car seat. Diaper bag was packed. All shoes were on the proper feet. Doors were locked. Lights, stove, television, radios were all turned off.

Then Dave went upstairs to grab something. On his way out of the room, he glanced at his computer. There was one e-mail, just one little e-mail he needed to answer.

As I waited downstairs, right by the door, three girls ready to go, things started to unravel.

First the baby started to cry.

Then a coat came off.

One child strayed to the living room.

A remote was found.

Mickey Mouse appeared on the TV.

By the time Dave returned, all momentum was lost.

We were perched at the moment, ready to embark on our adventure, and that one little e-mail ruined it.

When we tried to put the coat back on, one started crying because she couldn't see the TV. The baby's cry reached a pitch that only removing her from the car seat and giving her a bottle would solve. Upon seeing the bottle, the one not watching TV decided she was hungry too. Out came a snack . . . You get the picture.

Robyn LaChance of Sound Credit Union talks about how hard managing forward momentum can be with young children.

The other morning, my ten-month-old got up at five A.M. instead of six thirty. That in itself started the morning off on the wrong note. It really works best if I feed both kids at the same time, so I waited a little bit and then woke up my four-year-old. Being inclined to the dramatic, she pulled the covers over her head and cried, "Let me sleep!" So I told her I was going to dress the baby while she woke up. Oh, heavens! The ups and downs of a four-year-old are enough to stall any endeavor! She cried that she didn't want us to leave her. I said patiently, "Okay, we will stay in here while you get out of bed. So let's get out of bed." To which she replied, "Nooo, I have to stretch," and stretched theatrically. Finally, I got her out of bed and then she cried because she didn't want to wear jeans. I put a pink dress on her and her mood sharply lifted. She started twirling around, watching herself in the mirror. "I look so preeeettttttyyy," she gushed. The whole time, I'm trying to herd her downstairs.

The baby was starting to get fussy and I knew I wasn't going to be able to keep him occupied much longer, so I fed him and told my daughter that we were taking him to day care early and she and I would stop by Starbucks on the way to her pre-school.

I had visions of a nice little mommy-daughter treat in the car before preschool. Of course, the minute we dropped off the baby and got back into the car, she announced, "I have to poo-poo." No! I thought. I didn't want to get out of the car. But what can you do? And of course it's Seattle and it's raining. So we went into the Starbucks and it was another set of mood swings. First she didn't want me be in the bathroom with her. Then she got dis-tracted by naming the shapes of the tiles until she was singing happily as she sat on the toilet. Some-one tapped on the door so I tried to hurry her along, which did absolutely no good.

Eventually, we made it out of the bathroom and ordered our drinks. She got her apple juice and spilled it all over the floor. She was mortified and embarrassed, so I was mopping up spilled juice and trying to make her feel better.

Finally, new juice and scones were purchased and eaten, and we were ready to get to school. I was exhausted, and it wasn't even eight A.M. yet! Keep-

ing kids moving requires patience, creativity, firm-
ness, empathy, and stamina, and a sense of humor.

Actively managing the forward progress of your work
teams is similar. Momentum dies a silent death if not
carefully tended to.

How many times have you worked on a team that
is excited and enthusiastic about a project and one
person fails to complete a crucial step? Time passes,
folks move on to other projects. Open action items
linger. And finally, the project withers on the vine for
lack of support.

Meredith Weil recalls when she and her husband
built an addition to their house. "It was such a stressful process, and it seemed like the longer it went on the
more my husband and I argued about things, which
was so hard on our family. At work, when implementing a new product or system, I find that the organization and the strength of the project team deteriorate if
the project isn't completed within a reasonable time.
Because of this, I think ideally the deadline for a first
phase of a project shouldn't be more than a year (and
even a year is long). Ideally, any project should be broken up into smaller tasks. This helps people keep on
target but also provides a sense of forward momentum. Periodic check-ins and meeting deadlines at every
step are critical."

If you are leading a project team, pay special attention to momentum. Do not let one person start to un-
dermine the project because of her inability to follow

through. If one person starts falling behind, the whole group can fall apart.

Another momentum killer is distractions. Sheri Blumenthal tells of how the credit crises of 2007 and 2008 put a tremendous strain on her group. "It's hard to keep employees focused when there is so much going on. But we know we have deliverables, we know we have to get things done. I keep them on task by talking a little bit about their fears but then reminding them that, since we don't know what the future will bring, we must focus on doing the best job we possibly can with all the information we have today. I watch closely for signs of people who are emotionally checking out—taking longer lunches, on the phone more, leaving early, coming in late, that kind of thing—then I work on refocusing them to the task at hand."

Top 3 Take-Aways

1. Distractions are a major threat to momentum. Although you cannot eliminate distractions, you can remind people not to succumb to them.
2. Break large projects up into smaller targets. This keeps people on task and provides a sense of forward motion.
3. Lack of follow-through is another source of slowdown. If a team member is not doing his part on a project, correct him or remove him from the team.

24
Maintain a United Front

My husband, a freelance location manager, was working with a new production company when he overheard one side of this cell phone conversation between two equally ranked employees.

"Right. Well, I told him no."

Long pause.

"Well, the point is, if you tell him yes whenever I tell him no, he is going to come to you every time."

Another long pause.

"Okay, whatever."

The employee hung up and looked at my husband in frustration.

"You must have kids," my husband said to him.

The man laughed and said, "Yes, I do! And my colleague doesn't understand the slippery slope she is sliding down when she continues to do this with the team."

Parents understand the problems that arise when children learn they can pit one against the other. Even in the best parental relationships, there comes a time when, either knowingly or unknowingly, one parent says yes when the other parent wants to say no.

With my husband and me, this dilemma reared its ugly head in the middle of the night. We agree that the kids should sleep in their own beds. In the day, I can agree with this wholeheartedly. But at night, when I am in a sound sleep and wanting to stay that way, when those little feet pad down the hallway and into the room, I am more likely than not just to scoop her into our bed and keep on sleeping. Dave, on the other hand, is the diligent parent who patiently takes the wandering child back to her own bed and insists she stay there.

It didn't take our three-year-old long to figure out which side of the bed to visit in her late-night loneliness. In my effort to ease my short-term problem (staying asleep), I created a long-term issue (I am awakened every night).

Ah, the tricky three-legged race that is parenting . . . and sometimes managing. With corporations flattening their org charts and business models evolving at breakneck speed, it is often difficult to know exactly who can make what decision.

Tread lightly if you start to become the person who always says yes to underlings. It feels great to reward employees and it is hard to resist the urge to be the popular boss. But trust me, you don't want to be the one who gets woken up every night because you are the pushover. It eventually gets tiring.

I had the opportunity to sit down with two executives from the Seattle television station KCTS 9. Michal Jacob and Monica Ramsey told me of a time in their careers when they had drama within their ranks.

Monica: It was mostly just one person on the team.

Michal: She would come to me with something about Monica.

Monica: And then she would come to me with something about Michal!

Michal: We would always say, "Hmmm. . . . Let me talk with her." We always tried to stay on the same page so that we didn't get wrapped up in it. It's just like parenting. It's counterproductive if one parent is saying and doing things one way and the other is doing everything differently.

Monica: Yep, you have to be on the same page.

Danielle Weinstock, a television producer with more than thirty films and TV shows under her belt (including *Weeds, Crossing Jordan,* and *24*), as well as the book *Can This Elephant Curtsy on Cue? Life Lessons Learned on a Film Set for Women in Business,* talks about a time when she was producing an action adventure film and wasn't on the same page with the director.

We were filming a helicopter scene in Puerto Rico. The lead character was in trouble and the good guys were going to sweep down and get the bad guys. Well, we were running late and the location we were shooting at didn't want us there past a certain time and the helicopter pilot was getting agitated and things were becoming a little tense.

The director suggested that we put an actor in the pilot seat with the blades running to complete the scene more quickly.

Unwilling even to entertain the thought, I said no. I felt the safety risks were obvious and expected my decision to be universally supported.

I should have known that never works! Instead of speeding everything up, it slowed everything down by putting the director on the defensive. I had somehow expected her to read my mind. Had I approached it from the angle of explaining my concerns about safety followed by an open discussion, I think the director and I could have come to a solution quicker.

When you alienate someone, it's hard to get support for your decisions. But if you can bring people along with you, even if they are reluctant, you'll have that support you need.

This is especially important on a movie set, where things are moving quickly and there are a lot of strong personalities and tempers are often short. It's important for the key players to be behind a decision once it is imposed.

Top 3 Take-Aways

1. Do not become the manager employees know they can come to when they want something. Especially

avoid this if it earns you the reputation of being the executive who is the pushover.

2. Implement ways to keep in step with the others on your management team—good communication, extended understanding, or mutual respect.

3. Avoid alienating those people whom you need to support your decisions. Execution is easier with the support of your peers.

25

*Face It—They Are Not Going to Eat
Their Vegetables*

Making kids eat their vegetables has been a challenge
for mothers for many centuries. As Paula Spencer jokes
in *Momfidence!,* "It's become trendy to blame our
'toxic food environment' (in the words of one diet re-
searcher) for our veggie-rejecting kids. As if there were
a golden past when kids said, 'Please sir, may I have
some more kale?'" With all of the pervasive advertising, eye-catching packaging, and merchandise tie-ins
for processed foods, our generation does have a harder
time of it.

It's so hard to get kids to eat vegetables that Paula
Spencer devotes much of her book to encouraging
mothers to pick their battles and to leave the vegetable
battle alone.

Becky Fann, vice president and northwest region
executive for Safeco Insurance, lost the vegetable war.

"When my kids were little they never ate anything
green—*ever.* And you know, I was pretty sure I was

queen of my household. It was a summer day when my son was a little boy and I gave him, oh, I don't know, two green beans. I mean, it was nothing. And he wasn't going to eat those two green beans. We all finished our meals. I did the dishes. My husband went out and mowed the lawn. And my son was still sitting there. He must have sat there for two and a half hours staring at those two green beans. But I swear to God, I was going to win that battle, because what kind of mother would I be if my kids didn't eat any vegetables? Finally, at about nine thirty, he had a complete meltdown (he was only two, after all!). Now I was really mad because I realized I was actually not going to win this one. He was not going to eat his green beans.

I talked to his pediatrician, and she told me, "You are never going to win that battle, and why would you even attempt to?" After that I fed him as healthy as I could and let the rest go. It made mealtime far more pleasant for all of us. He's a grown man now and he turned out just fine—even without those two green beans!"

Many an experienced mom will tell you that picking your battles isn't just for the dinner table. It is often a vital survival technique at the office too.

Jeni Ward tells of a time she was faced with this type of predicament when she was teaching elementary school.

There was a woman at my school who had a much different classroom style than I did. She made up her classroom so neat and perfect. Me, I like to cover the walls with all of the kids' artwork. It looks messier, but the kids love it. That was okay until she and I got into a job-share arrangement and we had to share a classroom. I liked letting the kids be creative. She liked order. I would have preferred the room to be my way, but I realized quickly that it wasn't worth the fight. She took the classroom visuals and I took the lesson plans, and it worked out just fine. We were both flexible and we not only made it work, we actually enjoyed it.

Before I had kids, it would have really bugged me to let go of that part of my classroom. But after I had my daughter, I just thought, Who has time to worry about what the bulletin board looks like? Not the eight-year-olds in the class! I still try hard to do a really good job, but now I have a better understanding of what is important. The kids are important. The bulletin boards are not so important.

As mothers and managers, we have countless responsibilities. Numerous things require our attention, dedication, and advocacy. There is freedom in occasionally declaring, "That is not something I am going to worry about." Many women said that once they started letting some things go, they started to get along with other people better, they worried less, and things became easier. A large part of the letting-go process hinges on where our careers fit within our hierarchy of importance in our lives. While many women remain steadfastly dedicated to their careers and to their commitment to provide value, most internally start to view their career as secondary in importance once they have children. Most women will tell you that their family is the most important thing in their life and career is second—sometimes even a distant second.

This does not mean we contribute less than our childless counterparts or even that we care less. It just means that we have a different perspective. Sometimes, that perspective can prove to be healthier.

The financial industry faces huge challenges right now. My boss and I have tackled a few issues together. As a bachelor with no children, he approaches problems quite differently than I do. He will take an issue home with him and marinate in it for hours and hours, often completely through the night. I can't do that. Once I leave the office, I must turn my brainpower toward feeding three hungry toddlers, running baths, reading books, putting on pajamas, giving hugs, and getting everyone to sleep on time.

When both of us return to the office in the morning, my ideas for solutions are sometimes more innovative and useful, because I have taken time away from problems and manage to see them in a different light. History has many stories of inventors and scientists being hit with their aha! moment exactly when they were not focusing on a problem.

There is an undeniable power in leading a contextually rich life, and few things give context to a life like raising children.

"Before I had my son," confides Lara Garrett, whose company specializes in project management and consultation for high-tech events, "when there were problems I was working through for an event, it would really bother me even after the workday ended. I am such a perfectionist. I was so determined to do a good job, and the projects I managed for my events had to be as perfect as possible. But now that I have a family at home, I don't let it bother me as much. It puts it into perspective. Now I actually say, 'It's just an event. It is not the end of the world if something goes wrong.' I still do a good job and spend as much time working to resolve the issues. I just know that things will be fine and I don't dwell on it after hours like I did in the past."

Perspective hit Marty Taylor Collins in the face the morning she realized she forgot to fulfill her role as tooth fairy the night before.

"I realized then and there that no matter how important a title I have at Microsoft, or how many conferences I speak at or how many accolades I get, being a mom is my most important job." She wrote a poignant post about it in her blog, aptly titled "Confessions of a Lousy Mommy."

Today was one of the low-lights of my career as a parent. There are only a few times I can remember really feeling like I screwed up. One time was when left my 6-month-old daughter Taylor on the bed and she rolled off onto our hardwood floor. That was not a good day. Another one of those moments happened for me this morning.

My beautiful, precious son Christian lost a tooth last night. This is a big event in our house. It's his 2nd one. And he very carefully washed the tooth then put it in his special tooth fairy box, put the box under his pillow and went to sleep with dreams of the tooth fairy bringing him a prize in the morning. Of course 20 minutes after putting him to bed this completely went out of my head until this morning when he came into the kitchen where I was making his lunch and he had the saddest look on his face I had ever seen. Clutched in his hand is his baby tooth the tooth fairy never claimed last night. Instantly my heart sank. I felt like the pond scum below the pond scum. The lowest form of human life. I had just crushed my son's faith in the unexplainable, the mysterious and the magical. I made up some story about how the fairy was confused by his bunk beds and maybe she looked under the wrong pillow. He wasn't convinced and actually asked me if I was the tooth fairy. At this point the little bit of my heart that hadn't broken yet was shattered.

These are the days I feel like no other job is more important than being a mom!

The nightly eat-your-vegetables routine teaches us two things: (1) Choose your battles and (2) Keep everything in perspective.

Top 3 Take-Aways

1. Don't be afraid to say occasionally, "This is not a battle I choose to fight." You may very well find it extremely liberating.
2. If motherhood has brought you to a place in your life where you think, My job is not actually the be-all and end-all, rejoice! This can actually make you a more efficient, effective manager.
3. Having a family does not make you less of a contributor at the office. In fact, your family provides you with immeasurable attributes that make you more valuable.

26

Remember What They See in the Mirror

One night I was reading *Pat the Bunny* to Lexie.

When it came to the page with the mirror, she looked into it and gleefully cried, "Lekki!"

When she handed it to me, I looked into it and said, "Mommy!"

This disturbed her. "No, Mommy. Lekki," she said with furrowed brow.

I laughed. "Honey, it's a mirror. When you look into it, you see Lexie. When I look into it, I see Mommy."

She grabbed the book from me and took another look. "Lekki," she said with conviction and turned the page, closing the matter for the evening.

What you see when you look in the mirror seems like such an easy concept as an adult.

But is it?

We all fully understand the reflection when we ourselves look in the mirror. But do we ever really consider what others see when they look in the mirror?

Valerie Breunig, worldwide foundation executive director for the World Council of Credit Unions, recounts the time when she planned her four-year-old daughter's birthday party.

I grew up on a farm, so I had fond memories of farms. When my daughter was four, I was planning her birthday party and I had the idea of hosting the party on my sister's farm. My sister had five hundred cows! I figured it would be educational for the girls and they would love it as much as I remember loving it.

Unfortunately, as we were approaching, one of the little girls said, "It's stinky" (it was pretty stinky). Soon all the girls were holding their noses and chanting, "It's stinky, it's stinky." Needless to say, my daughter's birthday party was not the smashing success I dreamed it was going to be.

This definitely reminded me of the Platinum Rule: Do unto others as they want done onto them.

Just because I liked farms when I was little didn't mean all the little girls in my daughter's class would like them too. In fact, the exact opposite was true.

I should have stuck with the princess party.

Not only do we expect our children to like the same things we liked, we often invent the same expectations at the office. We expect others to perceive, respond to, and remember events exactly as we do.

One great example of imposing our own wishes on other people comes in terms of incentives. How often do we expect others to find motivation in exactly the same way we do?

I learned this lesson the hard way (and am still trying to learn it!), when I lost one of my best salespeople.

While getting my MBA, I took a sales management course from one of the best sales managers at Microsoft. He stressed the need to find out early what motivates a person. The best way to find out, he said, is simply to ask.

So I marched back to my office the following day and did just that.

I asked my staff, and my top salesperson said, "public recognition." I would have never have guessed this, for two reasons: She was seemingly shy and it's not what usually motivates me.

While I tried to give her recognition, I must admit that I often forgot or missed opportunities.

After she quit, I had to read through her archived e-mails to find a certain piece of information. The other things I found made me sad.

Every time I missed an opportunity to publicly recognize her, she sent an e-mail to a friend of hers. She described the accomplishment and the lack of praise and her disappointment.

It was a lesson hard learned for me.

On the flip side of that, a colleague told me an interesting story about one of his employees. At his company, they had a tradition of making a big deal of people's five-year milestones. One of his employees is so mortified by the public hoopla that she calls in sick every five years just to avoid it.

"Have you ever thought about *not* recognizing her?" I asked. It had not occurred to him to forgo the embarrassing ritual. "Everyone likes public praise," he said. "I don't get it."

And there's the rub. We don't get it.

Another thing ambitious managers often fail to recognize is that not everyone wants to get ahead.

Not everyone wants upward mobility on the organizational chart. And that's a good thing! There isn't a whole lot of room at the top. Companies live and breathe and thrive on the talented, caring people who remain in nonmanagement, nonleadership roles.

One caveat: Don't confuse being promoted with making more money. Numerous studies and common sense tell us that people want appreciation for a job well done and they particularly want that appreciation represented by periodically increasing wages. Just because someone on your team is not interested in moving up from his position does not mean he is content with little or slow pay increases.

How you should compensate folks who lack upward mobility has two schools of thought. Some companies cap a position's earning potential and require an employee to change jobs in order to make more money. Some companies continue to raise a person's salary year after year, as long as she is doing a good job.

This dilemma is especially prevalent in the banking

industry. Walk into any bank branch and you'll see the faces of very young, very inexperienced people. Visit the branch again and the faces will most likely be new, as the people you saw before have either left or been promoted out of the branch.

The bank teller is a perfect example of how the compensation question is tough. On the one hand, a financial institution may very well crumble if its entire frontline staff is making tremendous salaries. On the other hand, the teller is the face of the business. The teller *is* the bank to the customer. These lowest-paid, fastest-revolving positions can make or break the business.

It is easier to justify pay increases for employees who are making "progress" from one job to the next. It becomes more complicated to justify increases for those who find an entry-level position the perfect spot for them.

If you have control over salary philosophy at your company, I urge you to consider this: A good teller can recruit and retain far more customers (the lifeblood of any company) than most of your managers.

Compensation is one aspect of managing differently ambitioned people. You also need to provide support in other ways. Figure out and keep mental notes of those employees who are gunning for the corner office and those who are most happy staying put. They need a different management style over time.

Lydia Johnson, formerly vice president of sales for North America's second largest credit union, who now runs her own consulting business, had nearly one thousand people reporting to her at the financial institution. She laughs at the many times she dealt with people who were different from her.

Throughout my career I've managed a few people whom I was so impressed with, and I encouraged them to apply for promotions. I wanted to see them do well and be happy. Most of the time they would. But every once in a while I'd get an employee who wouldn't seek out the next opportunity. Early in my career, I was a little baffled and uncertain by this. I mean, I had my daughter when I was a teenager, so you can get a picture of how far I've come in this career.

But over time, I came to realize that some folks just don't want management positions and that is okay. It reminds me of a story about my grandson Aiden.

When he was about four, my daughter and her husband enrolled him in ski lessons. Well, he missed the first lesson and then he bounced around from one class to another before they got him in the right class. He didn't know anyone, and the class lasted from eight A.M. to two P.M. This was at Whistler, which is an overwhelming mountain to begin with. So, on about the third lesson, he and his dad are driving up to the mountain and he says, "Dad, I really don't want to go."

My son-in-law tells him, "Well, you have to finish what you started."

My grandson sat there for a minute and then said, "Dad, I think you want this for me more than I want this for me."

I sometimes think that managers want things for their employees more than the employees want it for themselves. It feels good to see your employees moving up. But every once in a while, you're gonna get an employee who doesn't care about that kind of stuff, and you just have to let it go.

Yes, employees are different. I could never in a million years understand how an accountant finds adding numbers to be professionally gratifying. Just like, I'm sure, an accountant doesn't understand how writing and speaking is personally fulfilling to me.

When it comes to motivating your team, don't look in the mirror to find the best incentive.

On the flip side of that, training yourself to step in front of another person's mirror can be an extremely powerful and useful discipline.

Marty Taylor Collins tells of the time she and her husband were trying to buy a new house.

We had been looking for months. We had put a few offers out there and lost to higher bidders. Finally, we found the perfect house for us, but there was another guy who wanted it as well. It was clear from the beginning that he had more money than we did. I think he even told the realtor, "Whatever they bid, put me down for five thousand more." But I remember when we had first looked at the house, the owner was fairly pregnant.

So I wrote her a long letter, describing how I had two young children and how I had done all of the research on schools and how perfect the house was for our family.

I remember when I was selling my house. I loved it so much that I wanted it to go to a good family. I was hoping that this woman felt the same way. I was also betting she was a little hormonal and emotional. I figured she'd respond to selling her house to a nice family over a guy who just wanted another investment property.

And I was right! She walked away from the extra few dollars to sell it to us. My husband was shocked.

But I knew. I had put myself in her shoes and I knew what she wanted to do.

In their bestselling book *Getting to Yes: Negotiating Agreement Without Giving In,* Roger Fisher and William Ury stress the importance of starting any negotiation process with the analysis stage. They advise you to step back and think of the other person—consider his problems, emotions, and interests. In other words, put yourself in his shoes for a moment.

A study done by Adam Galinsky of the Kellogg

School of Management at Northwestern University looked at two related approaches often used to understand an opponent in negogiations: perspective taking and empathy. Perspective taking is the ability to consider the world from someone else's viewpoint, whereas empathy is the power to connect emotionally. Although the terms are often used interchangeably, they are different.

The researchers found in a series of experiments that the group that consisted of perspective takers reached agreements 76 percent of the time, the empathizers struck deals 54 percent of the time, and the groups that did neither came to agreements only 39 percent of the time.

While perspective taking can certainly help you in your daily negotiations, empathy will make you a better boss over the life of your career. The first step to empathy is stepping in front of someone else's mirror.

Empathy is a key component of emotional intelligence. Professors at the University of New Hampshire define emotional intelligence as the ability to process emotional information and to use emotions to enhance thought. It is the capacity to perceive emotions, assimilate emotion-related feelings, understand the information of those emotions, and successfully manage them. Many people are starting to consider emotional intelligence a greater indicator of success than intellectual intelligence.

In a recent issue of *Fast Company* magazine, Robert

L. Joss, dean of the Stanford Graduate School of Business, said, "Over my lifetime and in my four years as dean, I've become more aware of and impressed by how much of leadership is about emotional intelligence. The more you lead, the more you understand just how much of it is about motivation—and motivation is about emotions. Most universities operate in the world of the intellect: The person with the best idea is the brightest. But to lead, being smart isn't sufficient. You have to connect with people, so that they want to help you move the organization forward."

The great news is that mothers have empathy oozing from our pores. We are empathy-making machines!

When I first met Kristi Larsen, senior marketing manager at Microsoft, her son was only a few months old.

I'm part of a group called Listening Moms. In one of our discussions we talked about why new moms have such a difficult time at the beginning. It is so that a mother builds empathy with her baby. I look at my little guy and he doesn't know what is going on and I feel the same way, and now we have this bond because we are feeling these same things at the same time.

I mean, I am a highly educated, accomplished woman, and the other day my husband asked me, "Would you like to nap or would you like to shower?" I actually responded, "I don't know. Will

you decide for me?" What the heck is that all about?
I can't even decide if I want to nap or shower?

When she told this story, all of the other moms in the
interview assured her that feeling would pass. But
there is no denying that living through that can make
us far more understanding of others.

Jeni Ward, who now teaches English as a second
language in middle school, tells of a time when a Russian student shared with her how scared he was to
present his science project. "He said, 'My heart beats
fast. I start sweating. I don't know what to do. The
teacher wants me to do this but I can't because I don't
understand her.' He was describing panic. I felt so bad
for him because I remember that was exactly how I
felt when I had my first baby and I know how absolutely awful it is to feel like that day after day. Having
experienced that panic myself I think makes me a better teacher for the whole class. I know what it's like
not to know what is going on."

For most of us, empathy frequently informs our
earliest days with our infants as we try to figure out
what they need, how to comfort and satisfy them. As
we practice this emotion again and again, it influences
our brains, perhaps explaining why researchers have
shown that parents' brains become more active than
those of nonparents at the sound of a baby crying. In
The Mommy Brain, Katherine Ellison quotes Michael
Merzenich, an expert on brain behavior: "The brain

changes when you adopt a new mode of behavior or begin operating from a different frame of logic, or become engaged in highly emotionally charged learning. All generate changes in brains that grow in strength as the behavior is practiced."

"I think being a mother has helped me tremendously in my career," says firefighter Theresa Paccagnan. "When we show up on an emergency medical call, my mothering instinct kicks in. It really kicks in when there are kids involved. I always take time to reassure people and explain what is going on. It's so important to keep everyone calm and keep the tone as nonstressful as possible."

Lest you sell empathy and its overriding principle of emotional intelligence short, let me give you some findings detailed in *The Mommy Brain*. Emotional intelligence, once viewed as a frill, is becoming more valued—and rewarded—on the job. "We've found that when workers have emotional intelligence, employers and coworkers see it as contributing to a positive environment, and it is correlated with important real-world outcomes—like getting a raise," says Peter Salovey, the Yale psychologist and emotional-intelligence expert.

Salovey and his colleagues collected direct evidence of this when they tested forty-four analysts and clerical employees from a Fortune 500 insurance firm on their emotional-intelligence abilities. They found the highest scorers had already received larger merit raises, held higher company rank, and received higher peer and supervisor ratings than their counterparts.

Other studies have found similar results. The most successful U.S. Air Force recruiters, for instance, turned out to score highest on a test of emotional intelligence. Veteran partners in a multinational consulting firm who scored high on an emotional-intelligence survey delivered $1.2 million more profit from their accounts than did the other partners. In jobs of medium complexity, such as those of salesclerks or mechanics, top EQ performers were found to be 85 percent more productive than workers of average emotional intelligence. In more complex jobs, such as insurance sales or account managers, the difference rose to 127 percent.

I find that the employment of empathy works best in times of conflict. I long ago made it my professional commitment to deal with problems head-on. When things get heated at work, I almost always give myself one full evening to think about confrontation before acting. In that "cooldown" evening, I discipline myself to do two things. First, I walk through the other person's situation in my mind's eye. Why is he acting this way? What is driving him to do this?

Second, I focus on what I would feel if someone were giving my message to me. How would I want to hear it? What word choices would make me feel valued and considered? What word choices would make me defensive and shut down my desire to reach a solution?

I craft my approach to heated topics based on those two perspectives. In most cases, it results in both parties walking away feeling like we resolved issues and salvaged relationships.

Perhaps the best compliment I ever received was from a coworker who told me that I am "disarmingly nice." While my "niceness" may be up for public debate, I do try to remember that you get more bees with sugar. I try hard to approach each conflict with reasonableness. And I know that when I am feeling especially angry, that is the time to turn up the diplomacy.

After all, the more you practice emotional intelligence, the better you become at it. The better at it you are, the more successful you will be in your job.

Top 3 Take-Aways

1. Never assume that others feel, act, appreciate, or perceive things the same way that you do.
2. If you don't know what another person thinks, believes, or values, ask.
3. Always seek to understand another person's perspective and intent when dealing with difficult situations.

Epilogue: Read All the Books,
Then Trust Your Mother's Intuition

I don't think I ever read as much on a topic as when my firstborn child was about to arrive. I knew with a certainty how I was going to raise her—no television, at least two power greens each day, rigid naptimes, and positively no tolerance for violent behavior.

These are all things that any book on raising small children advocates. They are wise words to live by.

But what happens when they are not?

At Rebekah's day-care center, there was a little boy named Bruce. Bruce was slightly older than the other two-year-olds. He was much bigger and far more aggressive. He was already showing signs of being a schoolyard bully. He threw loud tantrums and was rough with the other toddlers. And he just looked like a mean little kid.

One day, when I walked into the day care to pick up Rebekah, she was sitting in the time-out chair, crying. The teacher immediately told me she had bitten somebody. Bitten somebody! I couldn't believe my little angel would bite somebody. I was quickly planning my speech for the drive home. I knew what to say, I had read about this. Tell your child why it is wrong to bite someone. Explain that violence is unacceptable.

When we got in the car, I asked, "Bekah, did you bite someone?" to which she replied, "Bruce not get off me, Mommy. I said, get off, get off, get off and he not, Mommy. He sit on me and I cwied and cwied. Den my bites him."

Suddenly, it dawned on me. In a circumstance like that, I actually do want my daughter to bite the Bruces of this world. With total disregard for all of the pediatric books I had read, I looked in the rearview mirror at her and said, "As a rule, I don't want you to bite people. But today it was probably okay that you bit Bruce."

"Tank ew, Mommy," was her small reply from the backseat. This was three years ago and Bekah has never bitten another child.

Every book I had read, every expert I ever listened to said, "Don't let your child bite." But I knew, in my heart of hearts, that scolding my daughter was not the right thing to do.

Mother after mother I interviewed for this book told me of times when "they just knew." Julie Tempest, chair of the board of PCC Natural Markets, always knew when her baby was about to get sick. "My oldest daughter had six major ear infections. She never complained. I could just sense she was getting sick because her eyes weren't quite as bright and her laugh wasn't quite as raucous. I would know she was getting sick before she even had a fever."

Another mom said she just felt something was amiss on her way to the gym. She turned her car around and went back home, to find her teenage daughter in bed with her boyfriend.

And countless moms say they wake just moments before their babies wake at night.

Time and time again, moms just know.

It's important for managers to get educated; whether it is going to school, reading books, or attending workshops. Management has many complicated aspects. The more you can learn from others, the better you will be at it. Since earning my MBA, I have more knowledge to draw from when making decisions. I also have more confidence in my leadership abilities, even it if is simply the fact that I know what people are referring to when they throw around terms like "sunk costs," "barriers to entry," or "NEV."

However, even the best schools or management books will not fully prepare us for the real-life predicaments that we find at the office. But children, ah, children . . . children give us all sorts of practical training.

Our children can make us more human, more approachable. Children have the ability to loosen us up.

Michal Jacob tells the story of the first time she managed people.

I went from managing zero people to managing eighteen in sixty seconds! I went to Disney's school of Management and took the Franklin Covey courses. I had all these big binders and I was managing by the book. But things just weren't clicking with me and my new staff. It wasn't until we were at the company picnic, and my daughter, who was barely walking at the time, noticed this garbage can. Now, we were in Newport Beach, so this was a very clean, fancy garbage can with colorful stones embedded in it. She was drawn to these stones so much that she decided to try to put one in her mouth. I was talking to a few of my employees and I looked over, and without skipping a beat, I called to my daughter, "Honey, don't lick the garbage can." Then I turned back to my employees. That was the phrase that broke the ice. After telling my daughter not to lick the garbage can in front of my staff, they just seemed to like me more!

Raising children helps you roll with the punches.

Ellen Parlapiano, cofounder of Mompreneurs® Online, tells the funny story of her young son testing her ability to take one on the chin. "I was conducting a phone interview with a very important doctor. I was in a room on our second floor and the window was open and my kids were outside playing. I was talking with one eye on the kids and suddenly, my son took aim with his Super Soaker and accidently hit me full on! He drenched me! It was nearly impossible not to scream, 'You have to stop!' But I kept my cool. I don't think the doctor ever knew that I had just gotten a face full of water."

Raising kids help us keep our cool under pressure.

Theresa Paccagnan tells of the time her son slipped in the shower and cut his chin. "It was rattling. When we got to the hospital, they had to restrain my son on this short backboard. He was just a little guy and he was squirming too much for them to start putting the stitches in. As soon as the doctor performed the first stitch, it started bleeding. I looked at my son and said, 'Honey, that's what happens when a needle goes through skin—it bleeds. Everything is going to be okay.' "

Raising kids helps us think on our feet.

Janine Rush-Byers, of the Micron Technology Foundation in Idaho, had her house catch fire on Christmas Day. "My husband was cooking twenty pounds of prime rib for the thirty guests that were arriving. A spark must have caught the wall because suddenly he came in and said, 'The house is on fire.' I immediately told my sister to call 911. I grabbed the second extinguisher and started spraying. When it was obvious that wasn't going to work, I got my daughters and the dogs and sent them outside. As guests arrived, I gave them instructions. I asked one to keep everyone out of the house. I asked another to keep the girls warm in her car. I even asked another to go home and get a ham for the group! After the fifteen firemen hosed, pickaxed, and chain-sawed the wall, the fire was out and we went ahead with dinner. It wasn't until I was in bed that night that it hit me that my house had almost burned down and I still managed to feed thirty people."

Raising kids makes us appreciate the wonder in small things.

One of my favorite moms, Nicki Solie, a Cookie Lee entrepreneur, sent me an e-mail about her son. "When Trevor was eight, he was in TOPS soccer [a program for special needs], and one day he was the highest scorer of both teams. He scored two goals for his team and two goals for the other team. The other team won with a score of three to two. He totally enjoyed himself. I was, of course, very proud. It was a wonderful day."

Parenthood prepares us for management in a very real and meaningful way. The impact that raising children has on our learning is far more profound than any management guru or leadership book could ever be.

Steven Covey can't prescribe the right words to say to be accepted by your staff. Dale Carnegie training will not tell you what to do when the secretary confides that she is having an affair with your boss. *The One Minute Manager* won't cover how to act when you learn that HR publicly said something bad about your best salesperson and it got back to him. None of the classes in my MBA program discussed what to do when one quarter of your staff gets pregnant at the same time.

In the end, you have to trust your intuition. Mothers know a lot. CFO and pilot Brenda Morris says that her seven-year-old son once said, "If mommies got contacts, they would need to get four." It's no accident that the idiom "Mothers have eyes in the back of their heads" has prevailed for generations. We do know what is going on.

And we know what to do. Sometimes we don't have the confidence at the office to follow that little voice. Find that confidence. Centuries of evolution (or God) have given mothers a keen sense of knowing what to do. The responsibility of keeping our offspring alive has fallen on our shoulders for thousands of years. Women, particularly mothers, have an innate sense of direction when it comes to navigating through tricky situations. Use that sense of direction at the office. A mother's intuition is a powerful thing.

In *The Mommy Brain*, Katherine Ellison presents evidence that motherhood actually makes us smarter. She takes the commonly held belief that motherhood makes us lose our intellect and debunks it. Ellison identifies five attributes—perception, efficiency, resiliency, motivation, and social skills—that are enhanced through the process of giving birth to and raising children.

"It all relates to the brain maximizing the attachment to the young without much room for error," theorizes the neuroscientist Michael Merzenich. "It's analogous to the situation that arises whenever you're in a very high-stakes, life-threatening situation. The brain is specialized for quick, decisive action, at the expense of cogitation or learning. In a sense, the brain doesn't have *time* for complex cognitive stuff. It's all about protection, nurture, attachment, concentration on the over-riding task—and *focus!*"

Many of the women I spoke to for this book described how they were able to make important decisions quicker and with more confidence once they had children.

Lara Garrett tells of when she and her husband bought their last house. "When my son was three months old, we determined we needed to move. Before I had him, I would have spent so much time analyzing and agonizing over the decision. But as moms, we just have to make faster decisions. It's about survival. So when we figured out we needed to move, I made a few quick calculations and said, 'Let's do it. Let's buy this bigger house.' In a way, I felt more confident than I ever had in the past. I just knew I would get work. And it turned out to be true. I am making more money than I did before I had my son. The decision to move was the right one and I instinctively knew I could handle the risks."

These scientifically proven enhancements to our intellect will not do us much good, however, if we refuse to see them. Claude Steele, a Stanford University psychologist, coined the term "stereotype threat." Stereotype threat means that a member of a particular group, faced with a task thought to be poorly performed by members of that group, will consequently perform less well than he otherwise would on that task. Racial minorities, given expectations that they will test poorly on achievement tests, on average do so, as do women influenced by opinions that they will test poorly in math. Working mothers, burdened with negative stereotypes, may be similarly set up to fail.

The first step to defeating the stereotype threat is to stop believing it ourselves.

The things we face in the office are not complex. They are simple to us because we see them, experiment with them, and conquer them every day of our lives—with our children. Our children teach us about human nature. Our children teach us to think on our feet. Our children teach us what is important and what can wait. Our children teach us the infinite strength we have when we need it.

Now it is up to us to take the skills we are perfecting as mothers and apply them in our management roles. If we apply them with the same consistency and conviction that we do with our children, we will see success. As each of us starts to manage with better results, those around us will, in turn, see the whole category of working mother in a more favorable light.

As we become more comfortable in our own skins, so too will others become more comfortable with us. The more confidence that is espoused for working mothers, the smaller the wage gap and the greater the flexibility for mothers will become. This is a necessity in our culture. We must make it happen.

One of the best ways to bolster our self-confidence

is to realize that work and family are not mutually exclusive. In fact, they work in tandem to make you better at both. By understanding how motherhood enhances our management talents, we become more efficient at capitalizing on our strengths.

Now go out there and show them what you're made of.